Lernkrimi Englisch

THEFT AT DAWN

Sieger im Krimi-Schreibwettbewerb

Duncan Glan
Nach einer Idee von Bianca Mux

Compact Verlag

Bisher sind in dieser Reihe erschienen:
- Englisch GB/US, Business English: B1, B2
- Englisch, Französisch, Italienisch, Spanisch: B1, B2
- Deutsch: B1
- Sammelband Lernkrimi Englisch: B1/B2

In der Reihe Compact Lernkrimi Kurzkrimis sind erschienen:
- Englisch, Französisch, Italienisch, Spanisch: A2

In der Reihe Compact Lernkrimi History sind erschienen:
- Englisch: B1, B2

In der Reihe Compact Lernthriller sind erschienen:
- Englisch: B1, B2, Spanisch: B1

In der Reihe Compact Lernstory Mystery sind erschienen:
- Englisch: B1, B2

In der Reihe Compact Lernkrimi Hörbuch sind erschienen:
- Englisch: B1, B2, Business English: B2
- Französisch, Italienisch, Spanisch: B1

Lernziele:
- Grundwortschatz, Grammatik (A2, B1)
- Aufbauwortschatz, Konversation (B2)

In der Reihe Compact Schüler-Lernkrimi sind erschienen:
- Englisch, Französisch, Spanisch, Latein, Deutsch, Mathematik, Physik, Chemie

Weitere Titel sind in Vorbereitung.

Chefredaktion: Dr. Angela Sendlinger
Redaktion: Patrizia Ginocchio
Fachredaktion: Angela Billington
Produktion: Wolfram Friedrich
Titelillustration: Karl Knospe
Typographischer Entwurf: Maria Seidel
Umschlaggestaltung: Carsten Abelbeck

ISBN 978-3-8174-7638-1
7276384

Besuchen Sie uns im Internet: www.compactverlag.de, www.lernkrimi.de

Vorwort

Mit dem neuen, spannenden Compact Lernkrimi können Sie Ihre Englischkenntnisse auf schnelle und einfache Weise vertiefen, auffrischen und überprüfen.
Inspector Hudson erleichtert das Sprachtraining mit Action und Humor. Er und seine mysteriösen Kriminalfälle stehen im Mittelpunkt einer zusammenhängenden Story. Der Lernkrimi „Diebstahl im Morgengrauen“ ist die Siegerstory des großen Compact Krimi-Schreibwettbewerbs.
Der Krimi wird auf jeder Seite durch abwechslungsreiche und kurzweilige Übungen ergänzt, die das Lernen unterhaltsam und spannend machen.
Prüfen Sie Ihr Englisch in Lückentexten, Zuordnungs- und Übersetzungsaufgaben, in Buchstabenspielen und Kreuzworträtseln!
Ob im Bus oder in der Bahn, im Wartezimmer, zu Hause oder in der Mittagspause – das Sprachtraining im handlichen Format bietet die ideale Trainingsmöglichkeit für zwischendurch.
Schreiben Sie die Lösungen einfach ins Buch!
Die richtigen Antworten sind in einem eigenen Lösungsteil zusammengefasst.

Und nun kann die Spannung beginnen ...

Viel Spaß und Erfolg!

Die Ereignisse und die handelnden Personen in diesem Buch sind frei erfunden. Etwaige Ähnlichkeiten mit tatsächlichen Ereignissen oder lebenden Personen wären rein zufällig und unbeabsichtigt.

Inhalt

Story

James Hudson arbeitet als Inspector bei der legendären Polizeibehörde Scotland Yard. Er ist einer der fähigsten Männer und wird immer dann zu Rate gezogen, wenn seine Kollegen mal wieder vor einem Rätsel stehen. Diesmal sieht er sich mit einem ungewöhnlichen Fall konfrontiert:

Der erfolgreiche Krimiautor Geoffrey Auberon Carmody steht nach einer durchzechten Nacht vor einem Rätsel. Wem gehören der hochhackige, schwarze Damenschuh und die teure Unterwäsche in seiner Küche und wieso liegen im Flur schwarze Nylonstrümpfe? Doch damit nicht genug – wenige Zeit später bringt ihm ein Kurier eine Karte mit der rätselhaften Aufschrift Central/8.
Carmody beschließt den Rat von Inspector Hudson hinzuzuziehen, doch dann begibt er sich selber auf Spurensuche. Die rätselhafte Unbekannte entpuppt sich als junge und attraktive Frau, die nicht nur Carmodys Gefühlsleben ganz schön durcheinander bringt, sondern seine gesamte Existenz aufs Spiel setzt …

Geoffrey Auberon Carmody, a distinguished writer of crime novels, climbed out of the taxi with some difficulty. At his age, pub crawls which ended at discotheques, though great fun, tended to have a somewhat detrimental effect on his equilibrium. The early morning air was freezing cold, and the pavement was slippery with icy rain. Still, years of practice enabled Carmody to reach the door of his house with his dignity intact. Knowing that the only thing he needed at the moment was a good day's sleep, once inside he staggered directly upstairs. Had he been less preoccupied with safely climbing the stairs, he might have noticed a shadow moving in his living room. As it was, Carmody was relieved to finally reach his bed. Within seconds, he was fast asleep.

Übung 1: Lesen Sie weiter und setzen Sie die Verben in die richtige Zeitform! ***(decide, be, freeze, swallow, convince, meet, ache, awake)***

When he (1.) ______, it (2.) ______ shortly after lunchtime. His head (3.) ______, and walking to the bathroom he felt dizzy. One look in the bathroom mirror (4.) ______ Carmody that social calls were out of question. He (5.) ______ a couple of aspirins and (6.) ______ to make some really strong coffee. Lots of it. He had just begun descending the stairs, when his eyes (7.) ______ an extraordinary sight. He (8.) ______ on the third step.

There, on his landing, lay a pile of discarded clothes. Women's clothes. A black silk evening dress was carefully laid out, as if whoever had put it there hadn't wanted it to get wrinkled. Next to it lay silk stockings and expensive-looking undergarments, all neatly arranged. On top lay a single, black, high-heeled shoe. Of course, in the ordinary course of events, Carmody would have welcomed a woman of such impeccable taste undressing in his house, but he could not begin to imagine why she should have chosen the bottom of his stairs to do so. Whoever she was, though, he couldn't have thought of a more agreeable place for her to allow her exhibitionist instincts free rein. Unfortunately, Carmody was nearly positive he had come home alone. Puzzled, he decided to search downstairs for some answers.

ÜBUNG 2 !

Übung 2: Welches Wort ist das „schwarze Schaf"?
Unterstreichen Sie das nicht in die Reihe passende Wort!

1. mound, pile, stack, mind
2. night, afternoon, evening, midnight
3. impeccable, ferocious, perfect, flawless
4. exhibitionist, shy, introvert, timid
5. normal, ordinary, open, usual
6. consider, think, reflect, pond

What he found, however, was something even more bewildering. To be sure, after his activities the previous evening he would not have been surprised to see a few unusual things. A smiling pink elephant would have been absolutely normal. But the fact remained that despite his wide experience in the field, he had never yet hallucinated anything that came close to what he was seeing at that very moment. Spread out on his living room table, glinting in the winter light, was an assortment of delicately crafted jewels. Carmody saw about a dozen gold and silver rings softly shimmering. Next to them lay two ornate necklaces, half a dozen pendants, several earrings, pearls and a jewel-encrusted brooch. Carmody was no expert, but he thought these items looked genuine. It seemed that, for reasons he could not even begin to fathom, somebody's crown jewels had materialised in his living room.

Übung 3: Finden Sie das passende Gegenteil! Setzen Sie die richtige Ziffer ein!

ÜBUNG 3 !

1. materialise	☐ next
2. expert	☐ plain
3. ornate	☐ disappear
4. common	☐ amateur
5. expected	☐ bewildering
6. previous	☐ unusual

Of the owner there was apparently no trace, which was something of a disappointment for Carmody since he knew where her clothes were. A quick check once again convinced Carmody that he was quite alone in the house. The windows were still closed and locked, and there was no sign that a break-in had taken place. Carmody could feel that he was beginning to lose his concentration. I definitely need that coffee, he thought.

Half an hour later, he was sitting in his armchair with a large cup of coffee, thinking as hard as he could in his condition. He knew any reasonable person would have called the police. On the other hand, Carmody would have been gravely offended had anyone called him "reasonable". Moreover, he did not altogether like the idea of the police arriving at his house to find a hungover writer informing them that in his living room he had just found a small fortune in jewellery which appeared to have been left behind by some unidentified high-class stripper. And what she had worn upon leaving Carmody's home was also a mystery, since she had left behind her evening clothes – perhaps she had decided that the winter air would be good for her skin, he thought. Or perhaps she had made off in one of his suits. Something told Carmody that despite its obvious literary potential the police would not find this story the least bit amusing.

Übung 4: Lesen Sie weiter und fügen Sie die richtigen Präpositionen ein! ***(in, in, in, of, of, at, to)***

He remained seated (1.) in ______ his favourite armchair another few minutes, until the thought (2.) of ______ calling Inspector Hudson, (3.) at ______ Scotland Yard, popped into his head. He had called Hudson several times (4.) in ______ the past, in order to get details (5.) of ______ police methods and past crimes that might make his stories more realistic. He and Hudson had not exactly hit it off, however, possibly because one evening he had paid too much attention (6.) to ______ Hudson's friend, Elvira. But perhaps he should call Hudson just the same. He reached into his pocket and pulled out his mobile phone. It's right here, so I don't even have to go into the other room, he thought. Carmody looked up Hudson's home number (7.) in ______ his address book and dialled the number.

"Hudson."
"Inspector Hudson, this is Geoffrey Carmody. I wonder if I might have a word with you."
There was a sigh at the other end.
"I don't have time for you right now, Carmody."
"I understand, but I have something that might be of great interest to you. This afternoon, after waking up–"
"'This afternoon'? Stop there, Carmody, I have no time for this. I don't want to be impolite, but I have more important matters at hand. With all due respect I would ask you not to call me again. I wish you a good day."

Übung 5: Wie heißt das Wort auf Deutsch oder auf Englisch?

1. Beleidigung insult
2. unhöflich impolite
3. unidentified unbekannt
4. Anzug suit
5. gravely ernstlich
6. vernünftig reasonable

The phone went dead. Carmody thought of calling back and trying to tell Hudson the story before he had a chance to hang up again, but then he put his mobile phone down. This is going to be a riddle that I have to solve myself, he thought. He spent the next fifteen minutes carefully examining his treasure. The clothes were devoid of any laundry marks or labels which were always so helpful to the detectives in his books. Nor were there any telling engravings on the rings. Carmody noticed that there was no designer watch or anything at all which looked as though it came from the 20th century. This jewellery was old, family heirlooms perhaps, or even museum pieces. He fervently hoped it wasn't the latter. His only clue so far seemed to be that his night visitor had left behind one shoe – and one shoe only. As she – if it was a she, because he couldn't be absolutely certain it was – had done everything else with apparent care and precision, Carmody could only conclude that she had left the shoe behind deliberately. Had this mischievous Cinderella kept the second shoe as a sign of recognition? Carmody chuckled. He rather liked the idea of himself as a prince on a quest, though after ten hours of non-stop drinking he felt more like an old man than a prince.

Übung 6: Lesen Sie weiter und bilden Sie sinnvolle Wörter aus dem Buchstabenchaos!

He was not overly (1. rrespuisd) __________ when a short while later the (2.lloordeb) __________ rang and a courier handed him a (3. tteerl) __________. Cinderella had put too much (4. troffe) __________ into arranging the scene not to want to communicate with him. Carmody ripped open the (5. eeplevno) __________ and removed a postcard. He read it and (6. denwrfo) __________. In bold handwriting someone had written **Central/8** and nothing more.

What on earth is that supposed to mean? he wondered. Perplexed, Carmody turned the card over. It was one of those would-be artistic cards you buy in bookshops, a colour photograph of a single branch of a Japanese cherry tree. Against the dark wood, the white cherry blossoms stood out; raindrops were glistening in the sunlight. The photographer had obviously tried hard to create a particular atmosphere. This, thought Carmody sarcastically, is a card intended for secretaries with a taste for the esoteric – incense and Zen Buddhism. In the context of stray jewellery and mysteriously appearing underwear and clothing, it seemed very much out of place. For some time Carmody stood very still, racking his brains. When at last the solution struck him, it came so suddenly that he laughed aloud. What he was looking at were "petals on a wet black bough". He felt slightly ashamed that it had taken him so long to figure this one out. A poem by Ezra Pound had provided the title for his last novel, *Faces in the Crowd*. It was a short poem, consisting of only two lines:

The apparition of these faces in the crowd;
Petals on a wet, black bough.

Übung 7: Übersetzen Sie und enträtseln Sie das Lösungwort!

1. Blätter _ _ ☐ _ _ _
2. Ast _ _ ☐ _ _
3. Stiel _ ☐ _ _
4. Baumstamm _ _ _ _ _ _ ☐ _ _
5. Blüten _ _ _ _ _ _ ☐ _
6. Dornen _ _ _ _ ☐ _

Lösung: _ _ _ _ _ _

More significantly, the poem's title read "In a Station of the Metro". Remembering this, Carmody felt certain that his unknown lady-friend was asking him to take the underground, the Central line, and to go eight stations – but in which direction? In considerable excitement, he gripped his rucksack and coat, and made for the station, suddenly forgetting his hangover. He was beginning to like Cinderella's playful sense of humour.

I'll just have to try one direction and then the other until I see something interesting, he thought. He didn't have to wait long for the Central, but he was so busy wondering what other insanities the day might possibly bring that he almost missed the eighth station. At the very last moment, he woke from his musings and jumped onto the platform – minding the gap, as all the warnings requested – before the doors closed. He looked around. Nothing struck him as extraordinary. There was only the usual crowd of passengers, carrying plastic bags or rucksacks with their Saturday shopping. About the only thing of a criminal nature that Carmody could spot were the lurid colours of some umbrellas. There ought to be a law against pink in public, he thought.

Spotting nothing further of interest, he climbed the stairs. Outside a gust of rain blew in his face, but he didn't care. He had found what he had been looking for. On his right, there was a showcase displaying posters advertising various cultural events. Among them, a particularly colourful one stuck out. It was advertising a Christmas pantomime: Cinderella.

ÜBUNG 8 !

Übung 8: Wie lauten die Sätze in der richtigen Reihenfolge?

1. wrote stories simple he very

2. one late morning got home he

3. mean that does word what?

4. already the was he train on

5. off her all woman took a clothes

6. Cinderella woman is young a beautiful

The poster listed an address, so Carmody waved down a taxi. Fifteen minutes later, he stood in front of a multi-purpose hall which, according to the bronze plate next to its door, belonged to a church. Wondering what to do next, Carmody began to walk slowly round the building, taking in his surroundings. He had obviously come to an affluent part of the city. Around him stood large, neat houses with well-kept lawns and tasteful Christmas decorations. There were no garden gnomes anywhere, and expensive cars were parked in front of the houses. Carmody was on his second round when his attention was caught by something strange – something in the lawn next door looked almost like a cat, perhaps a kitten, but he could see no head. Curious, he went to investigate. Almost at it, he grinned. On one of the low walls that surrounded the front, in the shadow of an ornamental porch, stood a single, black, high-heeled shoe. He picked up the shoe and examined it: it was without a doubt the twin of the one in his house. He turned around.

So this is it, he thought. Glancing at the house, Carmody couldn't help feeling slightly disappointed. For the final destination of a treasure hunt, it seemed altogether too ordinary, smaller and less impressive than the other buildings around it. Still, he thought, I've come this far, I might as well see it through. She must live here. Walking up the garden path, he noticed that all the shutters were down. There were no sounds coming from the house. He rang the bell once, then a second time. Nobody answered. Hesitantly, he tried pushing the door. It opened. Uncomfortably aware that he was just crossing the line between a harmless lark and criminal behaviour, he entered.

ÜBUNG 9 !

Übung 9: Lesen Sie weiter und unterstreichen Sie die Wörter, die falsch geschrieben sind! Geben Sie die richtige Schreibweise an!

The house was dark. There was nobody to be seen or heard. Ignoring an increasing sense of unease, Carmody called out:
"Hello! Is there anybody here?"
Silents. He decided to risk turning on a light and found a light switch. In the bright light that suddenly came from a chamdelier, he saw that he was standing in a marble corridoor with inlaid mosaics. There were doors on both sides, and a staircase at the end. Large paintings on the wall depicted dark landscapes. On tiptoe, Carmody entered a room on the right which turned out to be the living room. There was no dout that whoever had furnished the room was not lacking in money. It looked like a picture from some glossy magazine on intereor decoration, but otherwise there was nothing of particular interest – no outstanding oil paintings or pieces of furniture. Carmody returned to the corridor. Looking around, he saw something he hadn't sported before. Hanging from the banisters, as if dropped carelessly, was a black silk scarf. Smiling despite the odd feeling in his stomache, Carmody collected the scarf and went up the stairs, where he came to three other rooms. The door to one

of them stood wide open. It was a bedroom, large and as luxurusly furnished as the living room downstairs. What immediately caught Carmody's eye, however, was not the wonderful antiq bed, nor the exquisite wooden table with matching chairs, but an oil painting of a nude stretched out on a divan. The painting was lying on the bed, but it was obvious that until recently it had hung on the wall right over the bed; you could see the spot on the wallpaper. In its rightful place, it had been used to hide a safe – a safe which was now open and conspicuously empty. On the pilow under the safe, Carmody saw something glitter. He took an involuntary step forward – and jumped back in fright.

1. ____________ 6. ____________

2. ____________ 7. ____________

3. ____________ 8. ____________

4. ____________ 9. ____________

5. ____________ 10. ____________

An ear-splitting howl filled the air. For a moment, Carmody stood frozen, unable to move, unable to think; he almost dropped the shoe and scarf from his hand. Then, with a rising sense of panic, he realised that the sound was a burglar alarm. He was now wide awake and completely sober, and within fractions of a second he understood the impossibility of his situation. He was standing in a strange house which had apparently been robbed, and it did not take much imagination to guess where, if the police caught him, they would find the loot. Carmody knew that interrogating officers were unlikely to be impressed by a tale which involved coded messages sent by a Cinderella leaving clothes all over London.

ÜBUNG 10 !

Übung 10: Beantworten Sie die Fragen zum Text!

1. What kind of novels does Geoffrey Carmody write?

2. What article of women's clothes (but not an undergarment) does Carmody notice on his stairs?

3. What colour is the item of clothes from question 2?

4. What kind of picture is on the postcard?

5. What animal does the shoe remind Carmody of?

6. The single shoe reminds Carmody of which character from a children's book?

As quickly as he could, he ran downstairs. The front door was still open, but the noise from the alarm would no doubt arouse the neighbours so he could never escape without notice. Hoping against hope for another exit, Carmody hurried towards the door next to the stairs and opened it. It led into what, had he had time to think about it, he would have called a smoking room. On one side, the room opened into a large, beautiful winter garden. Carmody had no eye for the lush green of the exotic plants, however. The only thing of interest to him was a door which led from the winter garden to a terrace. It stood slightly ajar. Without thinking, he pushed the door open with his elbow and ran out into the garden and into the shadow of the high hedge surrounding it. Looking frantically for an escape route, he eventually spotted another gate, practically hidden under a growth of ivy. It turned out to be closed. Carmody shook it violently, but the gate would not budge. Finally, he had no alternative but to climb over, an action complicated by the shoe in his hand. From the street behind him, he could hear police sirens approaching. He made one last effort and threw his leg over the gate and slipped down the other side.

Übung 11: Markieren Sie mit richtig ✔ oder falsch – !

ÜBUNG 11 !

1. Geoffrey Carmody comes home drunk. ☐
2. He wakes up later in the morning. ☐
3. He is intrigued by the single shoe in his house. ☐
4. He takes the tube to solve the mystery. ☐
5. The postcard refers to a poem in one of his books. ☐
6. Someone was in his house when he got home. ☐

He found himself on a small footpath leading along the garden hedges. Focused only on getting away as quickly as possible, he ran, thanking the fates for his relative physical fitness. Eventually, the footpath led to a border path surrounded by high trees. Carmody saw that he had come to a park. In the distance, he spotted a pond. Some children were feeding ducks; their squeals of delight could already be heard ringing through the cold air. He was completely out of breath, but there were a couple of joggers about, and nobody seemed to notice anything unusual – though a man carrying a single high-heeled shoe might be considered a bit peculiar. With his last strength, he walked to a nearby bench and sat down.

! ÜBUNG 12

Übung 12: Wie heißen die folgenden Tiere auf Deutsch?

1. duck ____________
2. eagle ____________
3. snake ____________
4. owl ____________
5. donkey ____________
6. squirrel ____________
7. mule ____________
8. bat ____________

It took nearly half an hour for Carmody to get his breath back and for his heart to stop beating like mad. At last, he got up. He began to slowly cross the park and find a way home from the opposite end. He was still weak-kneed, and he now had a vicious headache, but somewhere deep inside him and half suppressed he also felt something else. Was it triumph because of his escape? If the truth be told, that first rush of adrenaline had not been an altogether unpleasant sensation. Carmody was ashamed to admit it, but the simple fact was that he had thoroughly enjoyed the day's adventures – which were a bridge between his normal, quiet life and the life described in his books. And his narrow escape had only intensified his desire to find out how that jewellery had come to be in his living room. He walked on, throwing the shoe into the air and catching it.

Übung 13: Lesen Sie weiter und unterstreichen Sie die Wörter oder Wendungen im Text mit denselben Bedeutungen!
(across from, plunging in, observe, afterwards, excited, shattered)

ÜBUNG 13 !

An hour later, he was back on his doorstep. Tired and yet wound up, he did not notice the sports car parked opposite his front door. But when he had opened the door and entered, his ears pricked up. Music was coming from the living room. Somebody was playing his favourite CD, Genesis' *The Lamb Lies Down on Broadway*. Taking a deep breath, Carmody went into the room. He knew without asking who was in his living room.

"Hi, Cinderella", he said. "So nice to meet you".
A slender woman in her late twenties was sitting comfortably on his couch. She was wearing a black silk dress and a marvellous necklace Carmody knew all too well, having examined it carefully earlier that day. Her black silk stockings were shimmering in the lamplight. No shoes, though. There was no trace of nervousness about her. For all the calm she was showing, she might have been sitting on a sundeck at home rather than in the living room of someone she had almost sent to prison. Looking up from a book she had taken from his shelf, she smiled brightly.

Übung 14: Setzen Sie die Verben ins Simple Past!

ÜBUNG 14 !

1. cut ……………………
2. buy ……………………
3. seek ……………………
4. can ……………………

5. wear ______________________

6. stand ______________________

"Good afternoon, Mr Carmody", she said in a soft, deep voice, "I am glad to see you made it."

"Your shoe," Carmody said, leaning down and handing it to her.

"Thank you, darling," she said with a smile, laying it next to her on the couch. Carmody looked at her hard; he was thinking of playing the hard guy and slapping her face. She must have sensed this, so she added,

"I suppose I owe you an explanation."

The contrast between his excitement and this woman's sober and casual tone struck Carmody so hard that he had to fight not to burst into hysterical laughter. The next moment he began to feel his age.

"I don't know about you", he replied, trying to sound relaxed, "but I for one could do with a glass of wine."

"That would be lovely."

ÜBUNG 15 !

Übung 15: Lesen Sie weiter und fügen Sie jeweils die passenden Begriffe in die entsprechenden Lücken ein!
(dawn, tone, fetch, smile, real, handed)

He left the room to (1.) ______________ two glasses and a bottle of red wine. When he returned he (2.) ______________ her a glass and then sat down in his armchair and gave his guest an encouraging (3.) ______________.

"So, you are –?"

"My Name is Cornelia Thomas," she began in a matter-of-fact (4.) ________.

"Is that your (5.) ________ name?"

"It will do. I am, as you should have guessed by now, a thief. The house you were in earlier today belongs to a successful dentist and his wife; they are currently on holiday, skiing in Switzerland. I robbed it early this morning. (6.) ________ is my favourite time for a break-in.

Have you ever seen gold glinting in the soft light of a sunrise? It's unbelievably romantic. Anyway, I deactivated the alarm, took what I wanted and then prepared the house for you. After that, I came here.

As it was Saturday morning, I was quite certain that as usual you would be fast asleep, sleeping off the beer from last night. I spread out my trinkets. Then you gave me quite a shock by coming home much later than I had expected. That's not your usual style – to stay out until 7 a.m. Did something happen?"

"Oh, nothing important," Carmody said. "The discotheque closed a little earlier than usual. A funeral in the family somewhere in the north of England, I believe. So, some friends and I went to another club that doesn't believe in closing at all."

The young woman looked thoughtful.

"Bad luck. I should have been prepared for a late arrival. How careless of me. It's the details that always trip one up." She sipped at her glass. "Anyway, I was fortunate. You went straight off to bed and fell asleep, so I had all the time in the world to complete my arrangements. Did you like them?"

"Like them?" Carmody chuckled. "I've never been more baffled in my life. I applaud you."

ÜBUNG 16

Übung 16: Welche Gegenteile gehören zusammen?

1. important	☐ likeness
2. favourite	☐ easy
3. encourage	☐ calm
4. contrast	☐ stout
5. hard	☐ prickly
6. nervous	☐ detested
7. comfortable	☐ minor
8. slender	☐ deter

Cinderella nodded, pleased.

"I wanted you in on the game, and I knew that you wouldn't be able to resist a mystery as piquant as this. I'm a fan, Mr Carmody. I've read your books. I've been watching you, too. I was positive you'd rise to the challenge."

"And may I ask why you led me straight into a trap? I take it that you were the one who set off the alarm?"

"Naturally. Let us say, your little treasure hunt, apart from giving you an appetite, ensured me both your full attention and a good bargaining position, for I require your cooperation as well."

"My cooperation? I don't understand."

"You remember that glittering thing on the pillow under the safe?" she asked with a smile. "The brooch you saw this morning. You examined it carefully, didn't you? The police now have in their possession a piece of the swag which the burglar must have dropped in his haste. It has your fingerprints all over it."

Übung 17: Welches Wort ist das „schwarze Schaf"?

1. alarm, sound, siren, bell
2. treasure, trophy, booty, swag
3. consumption, notice, consideration, attention
4. thief, swindler, politician, shark
5. normal, usual, natural, sensual
6. nightspot, club, pub, discotheque

Carmody turned white. He started to speak but then said nothing.
"Of course, as you are a moral and upstanding citizen, despite your behaviour in discotheques, the police do not have the matching prints in their computer. Not yet. But a single phone call could take care of all that. You should also remember that the police believe the burglary took place this afternoon, at a time for which I, unlike you, have an alibi. All very neat, wouldn't you say?"
Against his will, Carmody was impressed.
"But why?" he asked, with a mixture of anger and admiration. "Don't tell me you went to all that trouble just to get my autograph."
Now it was Cinderella's turn to chuckle.
"Not quite. You see, I'm a successful business-woman, and my business is flourishing. Now, I'm looking to expand. I enjoy the practical aspects of burglary: entering a locked building or climbing through windows and balconies, deactivating various types of alarm systems, locating and opening safes, escaping unobserved and leaving behind no traces. I have sometimes even *re*activated alarm systems. I'm very thorough. My weakness, on the other hand, is planning – I don't see the weaknesses in my plans, hence I had no back-up plan in case of your early return. I simply lack imagination, I'm afraid. I need someone to work out unusual plans,

someone with a grasp of human psychology, someone who understands people and who can predict their unpredictable behaviour. Who better for that job than a writer of crime fiction?"

ÜBUNG 18 !

Übung 18: Lesen Sie weiter und unterstreichen Sie im folgenden Absatz die zehn überflüssigen Wörter!

Carmody's jaw dropped.
"You're telling to me that you want me to be your partner in crime?" he groaned. He couldn't believe in his ears.
"You could call it that", answered the Cinderella, completely unperturbed by Carmody's slow reaction. "It would be a 50/50 partnership, of course, beginning with today's percentage profits, since you are now at the very the least an accomplice. And I want to stress that it is burglaries not only: no violence, no weapons, no robbing helpless old women of their life savings. There are to some windfall profits, though: the burglary pays better than your publisher, the government won't take its share in taxes and its for entertainment value is considerable. It might also be a career move for you: it would give you more experience with the real world of crime, which you could then use in your novels."

Carmody was speechless. Suddenly, images of prison, the French Riviera, a sports car, bobbies with handcuffs, a beautiful woman, *this* beautiful woman at his side began to pass through his head. To his astonishment, Carmody found that, as outrageous as Cinderella's proposition certainly was, he could not honestly say he was not tempted. This afternoon *had* been fun; there was no denying it. He reflected on the alternatives, seeing himself getting old alone behind a computer, escaping the boredom with increasing amounts of alcohol. All things considered, he thought, Cinderella does seem to have a point.

Übung 19: Lesen Sie weiter und füllen Sie die Lücken mit den passenden Wörtern!
(like, deliberation, along, postpone, call, stick)

"May I (1.) __________ you Geoff?" she asked.

"I think we should (2.) ______________ with Mr Carmody and Cinderella."

"Cinderella? As you (3.) _____________," she said with a smile. "But we are going to be partners."

Carmody rose.

"This deserves a bit more (4.) __________", he said, "and I've had enough for one day. I suggest we (5.) __________ discussing details until my head is clearer. If I go (6.) __________ with it, however, there will be at least one condition," he said, looking at her seriously.

"What is it?" Cinderella asked.
"Next time you remove your clothes in my house, I insist on being present."
Cinderella smiled and rose, too. She walked out of the door, and without looking back walked a short distance to a shiny green sports car, got in and drove away.

"No alibi?" he said after watching Cinderella's car disappear from view. "I called Hudson this afternoon and tried to tell him that something strange had happened to me."
He walked into the living room, picked up Cinderella's nearly empty glass – and emptied it himself. Then he took his glass and hers into the kitchen. Suddenly he felt as if he had just stepped off the Tower of London. I called Hudson on my mobile phone, he said to himself. Out of pure laziness I called him on my mobile phone. I can't prove I was at home when I called him.

ÜBUNG 20

! *Übung 20: Beantworten Sie die Fragen zum Text!*

1. What is Cinderella's real name?

2. Did Cinderella set a trap for Carmody?

3. Did Carmody enjoy the "game" Cinderella played with him?

4. Is Carmody in good physical condition?

5. How old is Cinderella?

6. When is Cinderella's favourite time to rob a house?

The following morning, Carmody walked immediately to the closest newsagent and picked up copies of two London newspapers. Back home, he leafed through them, looking for mention of the robbery. Both papers carried short articles on it in the local section. One reported that the break-in took place around 2.30 p.m. The other said that someone had seen a man around the house early in the afternoon, but the description did not fit Carmody – as he had worn a green coat, not a black one – so he was relieved.

Übung 21: Wie lauten die Sätze in der richtigen Reihenfolge?

1. read the he newspapers always.

2. to dawn preferred houses she at rob.

3. Carmody Cinderella sent postcard a.

4. people older about getting worry.

5. thief you catch do a how?

6. good move career might a be it.

Two days later there was a ringing at the door.

"So, shall we stay here or do you want to go somewhere to talk about the future?"

Cinderella or Cornelia Thomas was standing in Carmody's doorway, speaking before he even had a chance to invite her in. He had thought of the young woman non-stop for the past forty-eight hours and was relieved to see her at last.

"Come in," he said, quickly, "I don't want anyone to see you."

"I'm not a wanted woman," she responded casually, and then entered.

"I wouldn't be too sure about that," he said, closing the door.

"Are you paying me a compliment?" she asked, a smile on her face.

Ignoring her question, he said,

"We could go for a pint or go to a café, whichever suits you best, Cinderella. We should go somewhere where we're both anonymous."

"Well, Mr Carmody, to be quite frank, I don't like to mix alcohol with planning – alcohol and business make for a bad mixture."

"A pint of bitter helps my thinking," he said and put on his coat.

"Not if your last book is anything to judge by."

"I nearly got an award for *Faces in the Crowd*."

"Writers always get awards for their worst books. Prize committees just try to make up for not noticing the best works when they first came out."

"You think *Faces in the Crowd* was my worst – ?"

"Yes, but don't take it so hard. Let's go somewhere for a coffee and maybe I'll treat you to dinner afterwards."

Übung 22: Lesen Sie weiter und unterstreichen Sie das passende Wort der zwei Varianten!

On the way to the underground station, they began to (1.) discuss/disturb the situation.

"(2.) So/For, you are looking to change your approach, shall we say?"

"In the past I've always robbed people who are not quite rich but (3.) already/almost. The risks are lower but so are the rewards."

"And now you want to go after the super-rich?"

"No, they're out of my (4.) list/league. I'm good at what I do, but the super-rich would be too much of a (5.) challenge/change." She led the way down to the trains. "They have better alarm systems and they usually have servants and maids – that sort of thing. The risk is simply too high for me."

"It's good to know your limits. So which group is to be your next (6.) seal/target?"

"The rich. People one step above those I've been targeting so far. Senior executives, board members, those will be the target."

"How long have you been in this 'business'?" he asked as the train pulled (7.) onto/into the station.

"Long enough," she answered, walking onto the train.

"That's not very specific."

"That's as specific as it gets."

The train was (8.) somehow/somewhat full.

"I'm trying to decide if I'm going to join you or not and – "

"The decision has already been made. Remember," she changed to a (9.) whisper/yell, "all I have to do is place one phone call and Geoffrey Auberon Carmody, best-selling crime writer, is sitting in police custody."

"You wouldn't."

"Trust me," she flashed a charming smile, "I would."
"Then I'd just tell the police everything I know," he whispered in her ear.
"Which is what, exactly?" she answered, raising her voice a little.
Carmody was silent for a moment.
"If you have such problems with planning, there's likely to be something to connect you to the job at the dentist's house."
"I have an alibi, remember? And there's enough to connect you to the house."
"It can't be any more real than anything I could come up with."
"But it can be. You see, my alibi has the virtue of being true."
Carmody said nothing further. He stood up straight and looked over her head at all the people around him. University students, mothers with children, a few businessmen and women. She pulled on the sleeve of his coat and he leaned down.
"I have no desire to see you in prison. I want to work with you."

! ÜBUNG 23

Übung 23: Welche Synonyme gehören zusammen?

1. help	☐ talk about
2. exact	☐ precise
3. charming	☐ delightful
4. limit	☐ boundary
5. discuss	☐ most recent
6. last	☐ aid

Carmody looked into her eyes and noticed that they were bright green. He felt himself swallowed up in them. It had been so long since he had been in a relationship with a woman that he was almost defenceless against those summer-grass-green eyes.

"We'll get off here," she said, and followed many other Londoners off the train. She led Carmody to a café on a side street that he had never noticed before. It was large and dark and targeted at a tourist clientele, which would ensure anonymity.

Übung 24: Lesen Sie weiter und unterstreichen Sie die acht Wörter, die falsch geschrieben sind! Geben Sie die richtige Schreibweise an!

ÜBUNG 24 !

She walked to a table in the back of the café and sat on a banch against the wall. Carmody tried to sit next to her but she painted towards the chair on the other side of the small bistro table. Through Carmody enjoyed his view, he usually prefered to sit where Cinderella was sitting. I'll have to make do, he thought, but I have to find a way to get the uper hand in this little game we're playing.

"So, are you making any plans at the moment?" Carmody asked carlessly.

"I'm always making plans," she responded. "You want to leave as little as possible to chance."

"Bringing in a parterre increases the risk."

"Naturally," she answered, "but I'm willing to take that risiko."

1.________ 2.________ 3.________ 4.________

5.________ 6.________ 7.________ 8.________

The waiter came over and took their order. Carmody wanted to order a pint of bitter but took a tea instead. They sat silently until the waiter came back with their order. She sipped at her café au lait and watched the waiter walk away, watched him rather closely, Carmody thought.

Übung 25: Welche Wörter gehören in die Lücken? Setzen Sie ein!
(challenge, throat, life, jealous, modern, partnership)

“I see he is more to your taste,” he said bitterly.

“You mustn’t be (1.) ____________, my dear Geoff – ”

“ – Mr Carmody,” he corrected.

“As you like. So, what do you wish to discuss? Our (2.) ____________?”

“You seem to have me by the, er, by the (3.) ________________,” Carmody said, not quite believing what he said.

“That won’t do at all,” she countered. “You should see this as a (4.) ___________, as a distraction from every-day (5.) ____________.”

“So, we’re to be the (6.) ____________ British Bonnie and Clyde, wanted all over England.”

“Remember, I said ‘No guns.’ I have no wish to end up the way they did. And, secondly, I don’t want to be ‘wanted.’ To be ‘wanted’ is no sign of success: it’s a sign of failure.”
“So, what is my role?”
“As I said, I want help in planning. I want to move into new territory, and I want some creative input from you.”
“I have no real experience.”
“Your novels seem to say otherwise. But that’s of no importance. I want your creativity, your ideas. Even in your weakest works, like *Faces in the Crowd*, there are ingenious crimes.”

Carmody turned red. He did not really believe *Faces* to be such a weak work, and to be criticized by someone whose admiration he longed for was also rather painful.

Übung 26: Unterstreichen Sie die englische Entsprechung der folgenden Substantive im Text!
(Zahnarzt, Schweiz, Vorschlag, Lösung, Forschung, Firmen, Zäune, Diener)

"So, you simply want me to make a suggestion? You want me to say, for instance, that we should target CEOs of small companies? We should try to get lists of flight passengers in business class where husbands and wives are seated together? We should sit outside nightclubs with the young and beautiful clientele?"
"You're losing your touch, Geoff. How do you think I found out about our dentist, for example? I got a passenger list for a flight to Switzerland. I expect you to come up with something different."
"Okay." Carmody sat there a moment, staring over Cinderella's head, at a wall with roses and fences. "Perhaps you should consider watching who goes to play polo. Find out who some of the single men are and visit their homes when they're playing polo."
"Not bad," she said, but without much interest.
"You would have to follow them home to find out where they live and if they have girlfriends or servants. That might take some time, so perhaps that's not the best solution."
"That's called 'research,' Geoff. If you want something to work flawlessly, then you have to prepare well, prepare even for the things you cannot predict. A polo player might fall and break a leg, for instance."

"But that's an opportunity," said Carmody. "If a player falls, he doesn't go home; he goes into hospital. Then you have all the time you need."

"Now that's a good idea. But," she said, looking towards the door leading outside,- "this isn't exactly the time of year for such a plan. It's cold, wet – in a few weeks it will be Christmas."

"Cinderella, my dear, the horses are there all-the-year-round, so there has to be a place where the players can practise even in the autumn and winter. The real difficulty is getting the player into hospital. It isn't every day that they fall off horses while playing, though it's always a possibility. It's what you might call an occupational hazard. Someone will have to make sure there's an accident – and then escape without arousing any suspicions."

"I will take care of that," she said coldly.

! ÜBUNG 27

Übung 27: Wie heißt der Plural der folgenden Substantive? Setzen Sie ein!

1. thief ....
2. journey ....
3. wife ....
4. child ....
5. body ....
6. novel ....
7. leaf ....
8. foot ....

Suddenly Carmody saw another side to the beautiful, young woman sitting opposite him. Her face was hard and though there was no gun in her hand, the look in her eyes made him glance at her hands to see what they were doing. As quickly as this moment came, it was gone.

"You've proven you still have what it takes," she said.

She paid for the coffee and the two got up to leave.

"I'm glad to hear you say that, Cinderella."

"But don't get overconfident," she warned as they stepped outside.

The smile left Carmody's face and he walked next to her, somehow smaller than her, though her head only reached up to his shoulders. He followed her to a restaurant where they ate Indian food. The mood was quiet and the conversation pleasant but superficial. When they left the restaurant, she offered him her hand and said she would be back in touch with him soon. Before he knew it, she was gone. He made his way to one of his usual pubs and stayed until closing time.

Übung 28: Welche Bedeutung haben folgende Redewendungen? Kreuzen Sie die richtige Lösung an!

ÜBUNG 28 !

1. to hit it off with someone
   a) ☐ to get in a fight with someone
   b) ☐ to start a project with someone
   c) ☐ to have a good relationship with someone

2. to have a word with someone
   a) ☐ to speak to someone
   b) ☐ to disagree with someone
   c) ☐ to go into a meeting with someone

3. to lend someone a hand
   a) ☐ to give someone some money
   b) ☐ to give someone a place to stay for the night
   c) ☐ to help someone

4. to rise to the challenge
   a) ☐ to get up with the alarm clock
   b) ☐ to perform well because you have to
   c) ☐ to try and be successful

5. to stick around
   a) ☐ to stay around
   b) ☐ to be in the way
   c) ☐ to enjoy doing something

6. to have someone by the throat
   a) ☐ to be ready to kill someone
   b) ☐ to help someone out with a problem
   c) ☐ someone is defenceless against you

The following morning, he lay in bed, feeling sorry for himself. You're getting yourself in trouble with her. For her. She's not Cinderella; she's my nemesis.

ÜBUNG 29 !

Übung 29: Geben Sie die zwei Steigerungsformen an!

1. rich ______________ ______________
2. good ______________ ______________
3. bad ______________ ______________

4. expensive ________ ________

5. many ________ ________

6. pretty ________ ________

Well, he thought, I haven't done anything illegal. I walked into that house thinking it was part of a practical joke and found out that it was something much more serious – but I didn't really *do* anything. And last night, I only outlined a possibility. If anyone overheard us, I could say that I was working on a new story. Then, he continued, I had better start working on that story. He got up, made a pot of tea, sat down at his computer and began to write. For two days he worked on the story, developing strategies for deciding who should be the target. He imagined scenarios at the polo stadium – someone shot at the player and that landed him in hospital; someone shot at the horse with the same result; someone ran onto the pitch and startled the horse, which threw its rider. Carmody was not pleased with any of these possibilities, but he was not worried either. It was all in fun, all theoretical; none of it had anything to do with the real world. It was pure amusement. At the end of the second day, he sat back after turning off his computer and crossed his arms, quite pleased with himself. What will I call this story? he wondered. Much of it was based on his own experiences of the past week but slightly modified.

ÜBUNG 30 !

Übung 30: Markieren Sie mit richtig ✔ oder falsch – !

1. Geoffrey Carmody trusts Cinderella completely. ☐
2. Cinderella wants to rob the richest people in the world. ☐
3. Carmody's ideas were not as good as Cinderella had hoped. ☐

4. Carmody believes he has done nothing wrong. ☐
5. Cinderella loved *Faces in the Crowd.* ☐
6. Carmody has begun a new novel. ☐

The following morning, the phone rang just as Carmody was preparing to sit down at the computer. The coffee was hot, the sun was shining in and he was congratulating himself that he had hardly thought of Cinderella, or Cornelia Thomas, as she called herself, the last two days. The story had taken off on its own. A third person joined the two conspirators and forced an accident on the pitch. Writing always took him away from the real world.

! ÜBUNG 31

Übung 31: Welches Wort ist das „schwarze Schaf"?

1. pleased, happy, content, satisfactory
2. illegal, probation, prohibited, unlawful
3. startled, surprised, upset, shocked
4. time, mood, atmosphere, tone
5. congratulate, praise, preserve, applaud
6. run into, meet, chance on, run onto

"Carmody."
"Hello, Geoff," said a familiar voice.
Her voice is silky smooth, he thought.
"Cinderella."
"Cornelia. Cornelia Thomas."
"What can I do for you?"
"I want you to meet me at Marylebone tube station."
"When should I meet you?"
"In an hour."

"And why exactly are we meeting?"
"Do you need a reason?"
"You *are* reason enough, Cinderella."
"I thought you might see it that way."

Übung 32: Setzen Sie die richtigen Präpositionen ein!
(on, in, of, for, by, with)

1. The store closes in five minutes. Can you get there ______ time?

2. I am ______ charge ______ five employees and a large budget.

3. I'm going to New York ______ business next week.

4. The Mayor is responsible ______ running the city government.

5. He went to work ______ spite ______ his cold.

6. The meeting starts at 9 a.m. Please be ______ time.

I'm not doing anything wrong, he told himself, on the tube taking him to Marylebone station. This is just for fun. The problem was that he was not sure if he was having fun anymore. Outside the station, the green sports car turned the corner off Harewood Avenue and came to a loud halt. Even before he opened the car door, he stopped wondering if he was having fun – it simply *was*. That luminous smile, the excitement of the car engine waiting to be set free, that body beneath the burgundy dress – so young, so beautiful, so powerful. Her smile as she offered him her cheek was enough to make him want to offer her his soul. He wanted to make it a long kiss, but she turned her face away to make sure no cars were coming up behind her, put the car in first gear and they shot into the street and onto Marylebone before he could even fasten his seatbelt.

Übung 33: Unterstreichen Sie die Wörter/Wendungen mit denselben Bedeutungen! ***(cosy, leisure, hurry, demanding, fancy, slight)***

"We seem to be in a bit of a rush," Carmody said, once comfortable and safely in his seat.
"We have a lot to do this morning, Geoff. This isn't about pleasure; we're going on business."
"I prefer a bit of pleasure with my business."
"You prefer a bit too much pleasure with your business," she corrected.
"You're rather hard, Neely."
"Can't you just call me by my first name?"
"I don't know your first name."

Cinderella pulled off the motorway and drove through a village. Just outside the village, they came upon a large, modern building with Corinthian columns that gave it a classical look but revealed little about its purpose.
"This is an indoor polo stadium. Guard's Crossing, it's called."
"About 45 minutes from central London, I believe," Carmody said. "But between central London and here there are several areas where the young and not-so-young men have their homes."
"So, what exactly are we doing here, Cinderella? Surely we didn't drive all this way just to look at a building?"
"Very good, Geoff. No, we didn't just drive here to turn around and go back into the city. And I didn't bring you here just because I wanted to spend some time with you. We're going to go inside and find out about membership."
"And we're going to go in as husband and wife?"
"Unless you have a better suggestion."
"I couldn't think of anything better in the world, darling."

Übung 34: Setzen Sie das passende Fragewort ein!

1. ______________ old is Geoffrey Carmody?
2. ______________ is the polo club located?
3. ______________ is the polo club called?
4. ______________ does Cinderella want to work with Carmody?
5. ______________ underground station did they meet at?
6. ______________ does Cinderella prefer to rob houses?

At that moment, Carmody knew that the past two days had been for nothing. He hadn't thought of Cinderella in that time, but as soon as he was in her presence she meant everything to him. She was a woman who knew what she wanted. Unfortunately, she didn't seem to want Carmody. But, he thought, there's always a chance. I'll show her how clever I am and then we can stop these silly games.

The manager, a Mr Thomas Doran, was unavailable but his assistant, an important young woman who did not provide her name, gave them a brief tour and overview of the stadium and the club's members. Cinderella and the assistant manager disliked each other immediately but neither expressed it openly. Less than 200 metres away were the horses' stables, the assistant said, concluding the tour. When Cinderella asked about membership fees, the assistant manager mentioned a sum that was well-beyond what Carmody could have paid, but his "partner" did not lose her smile for a second.

As cool as a cucumber, she asked,

"Is that the quarterly or yearly sum?"

"The yearly sum," answered the assistant with a venomous smile.

"Thank you, dear," Cinderella said, "I won't take up any more of your time."

ÜBUNG 35 !

Übung 35: Lesen Sie weiter und übersetzen Sie die vorgegebenen Wörter!

Carmody followed her outside. He'd remained (1. still) __________ for most of the tour, speaking only to answer Cinderella's (2. Fragen) __________.

"You're not thinking of joining, are you?" Carmody asked once they were a short (3. Entfernung) __________ away. Cinderella led him towards the stables, to check out their (4. Lage) __________, just in case the assistant manager took it upon herself to (5. beobachten) __________ their departure.

"It's nice that you're here to make sure I do nothing foolish, Geoff, but (6. echt) __________, I didn't make it this far because I'm thick." She turned around and started (7. in Richtung, zu) __________ the car.

"I don't think you're stupid, Cinderella. I just wasn't sure how much of a game this was for you. Investors will tell you that you have to spend money to make money."
"Hmmph," Cinderella answered. "This is no game."
"What did you think of the facility?"
"I think their members are right at the level we want. Some of these clubs are more expensive, more exclusive, but the people who play there have servants and staff and I've already told you I don't want to have to deal with all that."

Übung 36: Welche Wörter passen zusammen?

1. membership	☐ belt
2. club	☐ down
3. seat	☐ fees
4. tube	☐ members
5. sit	☐ joke
6. practical	☐ station

Changing the topic, Carmody asked:
"When was your last robbery, Cinderella?"
"A week ago."
"I mean – before that, when was the last one?"
"I'm only going to say that it was more than a year ago. Might have been two years; might have been five. The less you know about me, the better for you and for me if anything ever goes wrong. Got the idea?"
"A lot of preparation goes into these 'jobs,'" Carmody continued, ignoring the last sentence from Cinderella. "Impressive."
"Yes, there's a lot of preparation. If you don't want to get caught, then you find out as much as possible before you make your move. This time, however, the process is going to be a bit quicker."
"Why?"
"Because it is, Carmody, now stop asking all these questions."
"That's my job: to ask questions. That's what writers do."
"Your job is to stay out of my way. If I want your input, then I'll ask you for it. Trust me."
"Never." They got in the car and drove away. After a few minutes of silence, he asked,
"So why did you invite me along this morning?"

"Are you thick? It's a club for men only. Didn't you notice that? Women may work there, but they cannot be members." Carmody was silent. "That's just my luck," she added. "I get an alcoholic writer who doesn't notice anything. It's no wonder your sales are going down. The ideas may be better, but their implementation, their execution, is not nearly what it was ten years ago."

"And you're the expert?"

"In what I do, I am. If you see any areas that need improvement, please tell me."

"Your relations with others …"

"What do you know about that?" she asked, raising her voice. "You know nothing about me." They drove in silence for a while, and then she rested her hand on his knee and said,

"Let's go and get something to eat. How about a pub not far from here where you can get a pint and I can get a cup of tea?"

ÜBUNG 37 !

Übung 37: Lesen Sie weiter und füllen Sie die Lücken mit den passenden Wörtern!

(reckon, explosion, step x 2, leave, friendly, right, suitable, open)

In the pub, she became a bit more (1.) ____________ and Carmody became a bit more (2.) __________________ too. By the time they left, two pints later, Carmody had already forgotten her earlier (3.) ____________.

"When can I see you again?" he asked once they were both back in her car.

"When everything is ready for the next (4.) ____________."

"What is the next (5.) ______________?"

"What do you think it is?"

"I (6.) ______________ you have to decide upon a (7.) ______________ target."

"Exactly, my dear Carmody. You are so (8.) ______________. And how do we go about doing that?"

"First, you have to get a membership list for the club. But how will you do that?"

"(9.) ______________ it to me, I'll get the list."

"I want to help you, Cinderella", Carmody said. He knew it was the beer, but he could not stop himself. She was silent for a moment. "Please, Neely." She frowned at him. "Please, Cornelia," he corrected himself.

She smiled at him and he looked down at his feet, warm from the heat of the engine. The alcohol from the night before and the beer from lunch had relaxed him sufficiently that he was willing to risk something, anything – if only to impress her.

"If I were to ask you to get the list, how would you go about doing it?"

"Well, I might first try the direct approach. Just ask them."

"Why would they give you such a list, a list of people who are moderately wealthy?"

"I'm interested in joining the club. I'm a famous writer."

"Number one – how would being a famous writer help you? Number two and more importantly – shouldn't you do this anonymously?"

"Perhaps."

Übung 38: Welches Wort bedeutet das Gegenteil? Kreuzen Sie an!

1. important
   a) ☐ insolvent, b) ☐ intuition, c) ☐ inconsequential

2. willing
   a) ☐ responsible, b) ☐ reluctant, c) ☐ reliable

3. appease
   a) ☐ proscribe, b) ☐ provoke, c) ☐ promote

4. luck
   a) ☐ misfortune, b) ☐ mislead, c) ☐ mistake

5. expensive
   a) ☐ ecological, b) ☐ ecosystem, c) ☐ economical

After a moment of silence, he continued.
"Perhaps if I went there as a sales representative."
"That's a better suggestion. There are companies that provide sporting equipment to the players. If you came from one of the more established companies, you just might be able to get a membership list."
"Naturally."
"Of course, you would have to do a bit of acting. You'd have to change your appearance, since the assistant manager might recognize you, and you would have to act as if you knew the person you were talking to. The manager isn't simply going to hand over a list of members to you, but if you go there acting as if you and he are friends, have done business together in the past, then maybe you might convince him to give you a list."
"It couldn't hurt to try," he said.

Übung 39: Wie lauten die Sätze in der richtigen Reihenfolge?

1. get point point how you A from B to do?

2. sport a green she bright drives car.

3. 9 a.m. Thursday leave we at on

4. I the were would you I if accept job.

5. do anonymously you this should.

6. visit you London often do how?

Cinderella drove to Marylebone station and stopped the car.
"I'll be in touch," she said, indirectly inviting him to get out of the car.
"There is another option, Cinderella." He made no move to get out of the car. "I may not be as rich as the people you want to rob, but you could move in with me and you wouldn't need to commit any more robberies. We would be comfortable, and we would have enough money that we could go on holiday occasionally. You wouldn't have to take these risks anymore."
"That's an enticing offer," she smiled at him. "I'll have to think about it."

"Please do, because I mean it. Neely, I –"

"Out, Carmody. Get out at once." There was a sudden change in her tone and her look. He slowly got out of the car and then leaned down to look in. She flashed him her best smile. He closed the car door and watched her drive off. Her car recklessly turned a corner and was out of sight. Carmody walked to the underground station slowly.

ÜBUNG 40 !

Übung 40: Markieren Sie mit richtig ✔ oder falsch – !

1. The polo club allows female membership. ☐
2. Carmody and Cinderella agree to meet at a petrol station. ☐
3. Cinderella does not drink alcohol when she is working. ☐
4. Carmody immediately dislikes the assistant manager. ☐
5. During the tour of the polo club facilities, Carmody was chatty. ☐
6. Cinderella does not demand more active participation from Carmody. ☐

Though he woke with a hangover, Carmody set himself to work at the computer immediately. In the story, he began drawing up plans for the interview with the manager. First he looked up the names of companies that supplied uniforms, helmets, mallets and other equipment used in polo – Berenger & Bros. appeared to be one of the oldest in existence. Next he researched the polo stadium, Guard's Crossing. Then he selected a wig from a costume shop – a wig with curly brown hair that would cover his thinning, greying hair. The following day, he put on a suit and then made his way to the manager's office. Once there, he laughed and bluffed his way into the manager's trust. Though it was not immediately certain he would get the list, in the end he did. A triumph. Carmody sat back

and looked at the story. He was proud of himself, though he knew that it was not his best work, that the story was not even finished and that it was perhaps a bit too easy.
I can work on it again later, he said to himself. The important thing is to have the ideas written out. I can always re-work them later.

Übung 41: Lesen Sie weiter und unterstreichen Sie das passende Wort der beiden Varianten!

Using his ideas as a (1.) guard/guide, in the afternoon Carmody went to a shop (2.) specialised/speciality in costumes and was fitted for a wig. He (3.) chose/choose one with short curly hair that hinted at (4.) youngness/youth and a bit of liveliness. The fitting did not take long, but he had to return the following day to pick (5.) out/up the wig and to be shown how to put it on (6.) correctly/accurately. Next, he went to a men's clothing store and purchased a smart black suit with a burgundy tie. It was in the classical style, too, a bit conservative but just the thing that might be worn by a salesman from an (7.) ancient/old and established company. Finally, he bought a pair of shoes, Oxfords. The last few years, he had spent little money on anything but the (8.) basic/ground necessities of life and doing a bit of travelling. He loved suits but his suits had lost their sparkle – and like (9.) stares/stars, he needed to sparkle, if his plan were to work.

The phone rang.
"Carmody."
"Hello, Geoff. How are things?"
"Fine. I've just been looking in the newspaper to see if there are any reports about the robbery."

"Don't worry, Geoff, the police have no useful clues and your secret's safe with me."
"Hmm," Carmody said doubtfully. "Well, I'm just about prepared to go and meet the manager tomorrow. I've got a new suit and shoes. I'll look different too – I've got a wig that makes me look ten years younger."
"What company do you work for?"
"Um…"
"Geoff, you have to be able to answer that question immediately. It can't come as a surprise. You need to get your story straight quickly and practise it."
"Are you going to come over and help me?" he sounded happy at the prospect.
"I've got too much going on at the moment."
"I'll let you know how it goes," he said.
"How?"
"Why don't you give me your phone number and I'll call you as soon as I'm finished?"
"I don't like people to call me."
"I reckon you'll have to call me, then."

! ÜBUNG 42

Übung 42: Lesen Sie weiter und unterstreichen Sie im folgenden Absatz die zehn falsch geschriebenen Wörter! Geben Sie danach die richtige Schreibweise an!

Carmody imediatly got on the computer and began to reserch companies that prodused polo equipment. He found one, called *Three Kings*, that claimed – no surprise – to have served three kings, many more princes and thousands of royally. Had they changed their name twice already? he wandered. Now, so they claimed on their homepage, "We are affordable to you." Looking at their prices, Carmody didn't feel he was the "you" they were referring to, but he read through the company history, printed up a copy of their order forms and product lists and looked through the little bit of information pravided about the company struktur. One of the sales representatatives was called Michael Stewart, and Carmody thought the name suited him. When he had finished researching *Three Kings*, he did a bit of background investigation on the Guard's Crossing polo club. There was precious little information on the club, nothing about how long it had excited – the only real information was that they completed around the UK rather successfully.

1. ____________	6. ____________
2. ____________	7. ____________
3. ____________	8. ____________
4. ____________	9. ____________
5. ____________	10. ____________

Although it was unusual for him, Carmody stayed at home, allowed himself only one Martini and then studied the information he had collected. He knew he needed to demonstrate familiarity with the various products, and he had to be able to repeat his boss' name. It would also be good to know some of the company history and to occasionally include such information in anything he said.

ÜBUNG 43 !

Übung 43: Formulieren Sie die Sätze im Passiv!

1. Cinderella drove the car.

____

2. Cinderella made all the decisions.

3. Someone stole the painting.

4. Workers in China made this product.

5. An anonymous group took responsibility for the crime.

6. The British eat baked beans a lot.

Carmody did have second thoughts, at one point. Maybe I'm getting a bit more involved in this than I should, he thought. Nothing I've done so far could really be called aiding in a criminal act, but maybe this crosses the line. Still, even if I give Cinderella the list, what she does with it is up to her. I can't control that. But Carmody was left with the uncomfortable feeling that he was not quite telling himself the truth.

The following morning, impeccably dressed in his new clothes and looking quite natural in the new wig, he drove to the indoor polo stadium. Since his car was light blue and not the colour he thought appropriate for his current role, he parked it where it was not immediately visible from the front door. He walked confidently into the building. Once in the dark cool of the building, he walked directly to Mr Doran's office.

Übung 44: Welche Gegenteile gehören zusammen?

1. impeccably	☐ latter
2. natural	☐ ignorance
3. familiarity	☐ previous
4. royalty	☐ badly
5. following	☐ artificial
6. former	☐ peasants

Carmody was sweating. The assistant, he and Cinderella had very briefly spoken to only three days earlier, asked him what she could do for him.

"I'm here to see Mr Doran," he said confidently.

"Do you have an appointment?"

"An appointment?" he said. "Well, of course not. Mr Doran and I know each other far too well to require appointments."

The assistant looked as if she did not quite believe Carmody, but asked his name as she picked up a telephone.

"Michael Stewart."

"Mr Doran, there's a Michael Stewart here for you." There was a pause. "He says he knows you." Another pause. "As I said, he says he knows you and he's standing right here." Another pause. "Right, I'll send him in."

Übung 45: Unterstreichen Sie die Wörter oder Wendungen im Text mit denselben Bedeutungen!

(pounded, organizer, moment, alongside, newest, looked, begin, short, advantages, grudgingly)

She put the phone down.

"Right this way," she said, leading Carmody past computers and filing cabinets to a short hallway that took them to Mr Doran's office. She knocked, opened the door and said, "Mr Michael Stewart."

Carmody entered. Mr Doran was standing next to his desk in a suit that looked much like Carmody's. His black hair was perfectly in place. Carmody's short, curly hair was also perfectly in place, but appeared almost radical in comparison with Doran's hair.

"Thank you, Ms Hartley. What can I do for you, Mr Stewart?"

"Mr Stewart?" Carmody tried to laugh. "Hello, Thomas. How are things?"

"Things are fine," Doran answered, rather unwillingly.

"Am I catching you at a bad time?" Carmody asked.

"Not really. What company are you with?"

"What company am I with? That's a good one, Doran. *Three Kings*. I believe you've heard of us and of me. I was just stopping by to see you about something we've discussed in the past." Carmody went into a brief description of the latest products available from *Three Kings* and was about to launch into a discussion of the benefits for members of Guard's Crossing when Mr Doran interrupted him.

"I'm sorry, but what's your name again?"

"You're on a roll today. Michael Stewart." There was a pause and the two men looked at each other. "You don't honestly mean to say you don't remember me, do you?"

"Well, maybe I do. A little."

"Doran, Thomas, Tom –" Carmody was almost ready to try "Tommy", but something (an angel perhaps) told him that the fellow standing a short distance away from him had not been called Tommy since his youth – if he ever had been young.

"It has been several months since we last met, but I don't think people usually forget me so quickly."

"It does happen, though," Mr Doran responded. "Well, what can I do for you, Mr Stewart?"
"It's about something that we discussed back at the end of summer. You suggested I come back just before Christmas and here I am. I wanted to get the members of Guard's Crossing better acquainted with our products. We are the premier company in the world –"
"One of the premier companies," Doran interrupted.
"*The* premier company," Carmody insisted, "for polo equipment and we want to convince your players of that. We want to make our equipment available to them at a low cost, at below cost actually, so that this club might become known for our products in the future. This is something we've already discussed in some detail, Doran."
"And what is it you want from me? Please remind me, Mr Stewart."

Übung 46: Lesen Sie weiter und ordnen Sie die Buchstaben zu einem sinnvollen Wort!

ÜBUNG 46 !

Carmody smiled – or tried to smile – he wasn't sure if he had made any (1. ssegrorp) ____________ in gaining Doran's trust and was beginning to feel a bit insecure.

"Mr Stewart," he (2. edughla) ____________.

"Okay, I'll go along with your little (3. keoj) ____________. All I want from you, Mr Doran, is a list of (4. mmeebrs) ____________ so that I can forward them a copy of our (5. grspin) ____________ catalogue with these extra special (6. setar) ____________ just for them. No other person, no other club in the UK will receive such low prices as these, Mr Doran, I assure you."

"That's out of the question," Mr Doran said firmly.
"What is out of the question?"
"Giving you a list of our members."
"What do you mean that's out of the question?" Carmody answered. "We already talked about it. You've already agreed to it. It was settled months ago."
"Just the same, I cannot provide you a list of members."
"Why the blazes not? Three months ago, you could and today you cannot?"
"It is strictly against our policy to release such information to the general public."
"I am hardly the general public, Doran. I'm the person who makes sure your members are properly dressed and equipped to participate in the sport that gives your institution its business. Guard's Crossing is nothing without the sport that has historically relied upon us for the most modern and yet most classic equipment. When your players practise here or participate in tournaments elsewhere, it is *Three Kings* that makes sure they have the classic look required." Carmody stopped speaking and looked at his counterpart.

! ÜBUNG 47

Übung 47: Was bedeuten die Wörter auf Deutsch?

1. participate	☐ Gipfel
2. confident	☐ streng
3. progress	☐ teilnehmen

4. strict	☐	selbstsicher
5. peak	☐	Nachteil
6. disadvantage	☐	Fortschritt

Mr Doran walked around behind his desk and sat down. He looked at his hands, opened the top drawer of his desk and then smiled briefly at Carmody. He looked around his desk again, quite slowly, and then picked up the telephone.

"Ms Hartley, will you please escort Mr Stewart outside." He hung up the phone.

"I am insulted, Mr Doran, and your members will be most disagreeably surprised when they learn of the opportunity you have so disgracefully deprived them of." The young woman walked into the room, and Mr Carmody walked towards her.

"Good day, Mr Doran," he said as coldly and as proudly as possible.

Übung 48: Welches Wort ist das „schwarze Schaf"?

ÜBUNG 48

1. cheek, courage, nerve, impertinence
2. chance, brake, opportunity, possibility
3. cabinet, desk, table, counter
4. mobile, telephone, handy, cellular
5. record, list, directory, file
6. do, accompany, escort, conduct

They walked together out of Doran's office, back down the short hallway and to the spot where she had first met "Michael Stewart."

"You needn't come with me any further. I can find my way out without any difficulty. I've been here often enough, but I won't be coming back, I can tell you that."

Carmody walked to the doors that led between the Corinthian columns. His legs were so weak that the walk to his car seemed a marathon. Once inside, he sat a moment, then started his car. Nothing crossed his mind, at first. He did not think of Mr Doran or what had just taken place; he did not think of Cinderella; he did not think of the wig he was wearing, which was now itchy, or the suit. He backed his car out without looking and drove away. He got onto the motorway and started back to London. After ten minutes, though, he exited and found a quiet park set on the border of an affluent neighbourhood. He looked around a moment, then turned off the car and started to cry. He did not really think about why he was crying – he just cried. Long and passionately he cried. He ripped the wig off his head and threw it into the back of the car with all his might and then rubbed his hands back and forth across his damp scalp.

ÜBUNG 49 !

Übung 49: Korrigieren Sie die Fehler!

1. Geoffrey Carmody writes always on his computer.

2. He drives every day to work.

3. She is working as a thief full-time.

4. We have been to Manchester last month.

5. Carmody won many awards.

6. They are immediately needing new uniforms.

Finally, Carmody began to drive again. He was totally humiliated. No negative review, no destructive criticism of one of his books or short stories had ever affected him the way this twenty-five minute ordeal had. How can I tell Cinderella I failed? he wondered. He knew he would hide the humiliating aspects as much as possible, but at forty-one he felt himself to be such a leaky ship that he knew she would hear the humiliation in his words.

Übung 50: Beantworten Sie die Fragen zum Text!

1. Why does Carmody get a wig?

2. What company does Carmody say he works for?

3. Does Cinderella ask Carmody to get the list for her?

4. What name does Carmody almost use on Mr Doran?

5. Is Carmody upset after his attempt to get the list fails?

6. How is Carmody supposed to contact Cinderella?

....

Back home, he fixed himself a strong drink. I might just as well have finished off a fifth of gin last night, he thought, for all the good it did to stay sober. After a second drink, his nerves were calmer and he had slowly begun to sink into a warm pool of self-pity. By the time Cinderella phoned around 4 pm, his mood was somewhat lighter and he was able to report the news of his failure without appearing wounded by it.

! ÜBUNG 51

Übung 51: Lesen Sie weiter und füllen Sie die passenden Wörter in die Lücken! ***(whole, tell, concluded, events, worry, sound)***

"You don't (1.) .... surprised at my failure," Carmody said.

"You can never (2.) .... when charm will work and when it won't," she responded.

"He looked more like a surgeon than a club manager, Cinderella. It's hard to believe he works with (3.) ...., living people. He looked more like the kind of person who deals only with parts of people – internal organs, bones, tumours, psychoses and the like. So", he (4.) ...., "what do we do now? How are we going to get the list?"

"Don't (5.) __________ about it", Cinderella said, "we've already got the list."

"We – you already have the list?!"

"Well of course, darling. I have the list of members as well as a schedule of (6.) __________. We shall need both."

"Then what was the point in sending me all the way out there to meet with Doran?"
"You wanted to do your part, so I let you. What's the harm in that?"
"I wanted to do something necessary," Carmody answered.
"Carmody, I've always got a plan B – I'm not going to sit at home and wait for you to deliver. And, besides, you never know who you can depend on."
"You know you can depend on me," Carmody said.
"Did you get me the list, Geoff?" Her voice was suddenly harsh. "Can you get it to me in the next couple of hours?"
"Well, no," Carmody answered quietly.
"Time is everything, Carmody. I can't wait forever."
"What is the hurry?"
"There is no hurry, Geoff. I just want this project to go off as planned."
"Do you have a timeline for this next 'project' of yours?" he asked quietly.
"This project of *ours*, you mean. Yes, I do."
"Will you tell me what it is?"
"Not right now."
Once off the phone, Carmody proceeded to finish off the bottle of gin, which was already less than half full, and he then went out to the pub.

ÜBUNG 52 !

Übung 52: Lesen Sie weiter und unterstreichen Sie die englische Übersetzung der folgenden Wörter!
(1. aushalten, 2. verschönern, 3. genau, 4. einschließlich, 5. Kätzchen, 6. widmen, 7. entfernen)

The following morning was brutal, but it was not as bad as some mornings Carmody had endured in the past. He got up and made himself a pot of tea, forced down a bowl of salty porridge and then sat down at the computer. He typed in everything that had happened the previous day in connection with Cinderella. He did not embellish anything. He recorded events exactly as he remembered them, including the wig that had failed and was now a particular focus for his shame. He could see it lying there like a dead kitten in the back of his car. If only someone else would take on the job of retrieving the kitten. He would dedicate his next story – this story! – to who-ever would remove it from his car.

ÜBUNG 53 !

Übung 53: Haben die Wörter eine ähnliche Bedeutung? Markieren Sie mit richtig ✔ oder falsch – !

1. proceeds/profit ☐
2. projected/targeted ☐
3. queue/snake ☐
4. rash/hurry ☐
5. harsh/mean ☐
6. peoples/tribes ☐
7. lighter/gentler ☐

Once he had finished with the story for the day, he began to wonder how Cinderella had got the list – as well as a schedule of events.

Surely she had not driven out there herself and charmed the list and the schedule from Mr Doran or his assistant. Even she could not have broken through, certainly not when Carmody had been there first. There were only two possibilities. Either she had got the material from a member or she had got it with the computer and was, apparently, an accomplished hacker. It must be one of the two, he thought. He could easily imagine her following a young club member home and seducing him and thus gaining access to the necessary information. Just as easily, he could see her at her computer working away. He did not have a clear idea of what "hacking" involved, but he had no doubt that if at some time in the past Cinderella had wanted to become an expert at it then she *was* an expert at it. Though he thought the second possibility the more likely one, the first possibility made him sweat. He wanted Cinderella for himself. How angry he was now that he had no way to contact her. I'm just a fox with my paw caught in a trap, he thought. To break free from her, he knew he would have to chew off an arm or a leg and perhaps both. In the meantime, he would have to wait for her to call, wait for her to breathe the perfume of her life into his lungs and make him whole once again.

Übung 54: Lesen Sie weiter und unterstreichen Sie die fünf inhaltlich nicht dazugehörigen Sätze!

The following day, she phoned late in the morning. It was now about 3.15 p.m.

"Hello, Geoff. Have you recovered from your encounter with Mr Doran?"

"What do you mean, have I recovered? I was searching for sunken treasure."

"Every time –" she yelled suddenly and then went silent.

"What do you mean, 'every time'?" Carmody asked. He could hear that she was still on the line but knew nothing more.
"Nothing, darling, nothing," she said at last. "I know that you bought a new suit and shoes and then you were not successful. And you bought a swim-suit and a swimming pool as a Christmas present. I just hope that you are not still thinking about it."
"I've quite recovered in that respect."
"In what respect have you not recovered?"
"I would like very much to see you, Cinderella."
"That can be arranged. Later." She hung up and Carmody was left with silence and then the hum of the phone line. Maybe I'll tape my Christmas cards up on the walls, he thought.
She's going to push me too far one of these days, he thought. But he knew that she would have to push much harder, and do much more damage, in order to drive him away. I should take a walk, down on the beach at the Prince of Wales' castle.

"Some bubbly?" Cinderella asked from the shadows.
"How did you get in?" Carmody asked, sitting up in bed.
"That's a trade secret," she answered. "It stinks in here. You drank like a fish last night. Oh, it smells horrible." She waved her hand in front of her face. "It may be cold outside, but I have to open a window before I suffocate."
Cinderella walked over to the bedroom window, pushed the curtains aside, and opened a window. The bright light and the cold air quickly invaded the room.
"Please close the curtains," he said weakly. "I can't take that light."
"If I close the curtains," she answered, "then we won't get any more fresh air and I'll choke. Besides," she continued, "you need to get up. It's ten in the morning and time for you to be up and about. I'll meet you in the kitchen in five minutes."

Übung 55: Lesen Sie weiter und fügen Sie die richtigen Präpositionen ein! ***(to, to, for, for, in, of, of, of, onto)***

ÜBUNG 55 !

Cinderella left the room and went down (1.) ______ the kitchen. She put the bottle (2.) ______ champagne into the fridge and looked round (3.) ______ some food for breakfast but found nothing that she could cook. After 15 minutes and still no sign (4.) ______ Carmody, she filled a big glass with water and went back up the stairs (5.) ______ his bedroom. Carmody lay (6.) ______ bed still, fast asleep again. She watched him (7.) ______ twenty or thirty seconds, the rise and fall (8.) ______ his chest, his open mouth, then she threw the water directly (9.) ______ his face.

"What the –" he yelled.
"Get out of bed, Geoff. I said 'Get up,' and I meant it."
"You don't give me orders," he snarled.
"Yes, I do. We're partners, and I want you up now. Remember, all I have to do is make one little phone call and you'll no longer be my partner and you'll no longer be a free man either." Softening her voice, she added, "You need to cut back on alcohol, Geoff. You're no good to anyone as you are now, and it's a shame if you don't know that."

ÜBUNG 56 !

Übung 56: Welche englischen Wörter sind gemeint?

1. something you know that you do not tell others

______

2. means that something smells terrible

3. people who work together are this (not colleagues)

4. when you cannot breathe

5. an army crosses the border and enters another country

6. bubbly

7. the material that hangs in front of windows to keep a room dark

Carmody threw his legs over the side of the bed and sat up. He reached under the pillow for his pyjamas and wiped his face. Suddenly, he became conscious of just how bad he looked. The hair on his chest was long and turning grey, and his belly was resting on his lap. Usually he hid inside suits and jackets and loose-fitting shirts, but Cinderella's visit had caught him by surprise. This is *just* the sort of body, he thought, that a beautiful, young woman like Cinderella will find attractive. He stood up and quickly walked to the bedroom door to retrieve his bathrobe.

"If you're going to quaff alcohol and beer while we're working together, you'll have to get used to the idea of getting over your hangovers somewhere other than your bed. You can't just sleep it off."

Übung 57: Für das englische Wort gibt es verschiedene Übersetzungsmöglichkeiten. Setzen Sie ein!

ÜBUNG 57 !

1. to turn ______ ______
2. to rest ______ ______
3. to call ______ ______
4. little ______ ______
5. chest ______ ______
6. to reach ______ ______

Carmody grumbled but did not say anything. He led the way down to the kitchen.

"Where's the bubbly?" he asked.

"I put it away. You don't need anything with alcohol in it."

"That would be the best thing for me", he responded, "something to help me over the –"

"Find something else," she interrupted.

"Would you like some tea?" he offered.

"I'd love some." Her voice became kinder.

Übung 58: Welche der beiden Varianten ist die richtige? Unterstreichen Sie!

ÜBUNG 58 !

Carmody put the kettle on to (1.) cook/boil and Cinderella went about cleaning out the tea (2.) pot/cooker. She opened several cupboards before she found the tea. Carmody watched her at work. He looked at her frail shoulders as she opened (3.) cupboards/shoehorns here and there, looking for things he could have directed her to. It was

hard (4.) of/for him to believe that she was such a (5.) though/tough woman, when at that moment she looked physically weak.
She turned (6.) around/up suddenly and faced him.
"What are you looking at?" she asked (7.) harshly/gently. "Haven't you got something else to do? You need food; you need something in your stomach (8.) for/after last night."

Without a word, Carmody went about putting together something to eat. He opened a can of baked beans, pinto beans in tomato sauce, and poured it into a pan to warm. Then, he got some bread out and toasted it.
"Here," Cinderella said, reaching a cup of tea towards him.
"Excellent."
"I can make a cup of tea, can't I?" she smiled.
"And I can cook."
"If opening a tin and toasting bread is your idea of cooking," Cinderella said, shaking her head, "then I hope you eat out at restaurants a lot."
He finished his first cup of tea, sat down and ate his toast and beans with a second cup of tea.

! ÜBUNG 59

*Übung 59: Setzen Sie jeweils **for** oder **since** in die Lücke ein!*

1. He has lived in London _____ twenty years.
2. She has been a thief _____ childhood.
3. They have know each other _____ nearly four weeks.
4. He has worked on the story _____ August.
5. We had been at the beach _____ the sun rose that morning.

6. The computer has been working on the problem ____ most of the morning.

When he was finished, he asked, "So what's the plan for the day?"
"We're going to go to Guard's Crossing and watch who drives up. There's a practice this afternoon at 3 p.m. We'll sit there a while and then follow someone home."
"You're not going to rob someone today, are you?"
"*We're* not going to rob anyone today. *We're* just doing research."
"I have to go to the loo before we leave," he said.
"Me too."
"Shall I drive?" Carmody asked at the door.
"After everything you drank last night, I think it's best if I drive."
She smiled at Carmody and led him to her car, parked a short distance away on another street.

Übung 60: Beantworten Sie die Fragen zum Text!

ÜBUNG 60 !

1. Why is Carmody's visit with Mr Doran unsuccessful?

____

2. How does Carmody find out that Cinderella has the list?

____

3. How does Carmody recover from the stress of his meeting with Doran?

____

4. What does Cinderella throw at Carmody to wake him up?

____

5. For breakfast, Carmody opens a can of what?

6. Does Cinderella admire Carmody's cooking abilities?

They were on the motorway heading north.

"How are you going to decide who to follow home?" Carmody asked. "Are you just going to base it on good looks, for example?"

"Is that what you really think, Carmody? If I were interested in good looks, I probably wouldn't be in a car with you, now would I?"

"Fair enough," he admitted.

"What would one of your detectives or one of your criminals look for?"

"I imagine," he answered, "one would look at the make of car, for instance. Is it an expensive sports car or foreign import or a luxury car? Perhaps the clothing, too. The walk – an arrogant walk, an I'm-king-of-the-forest walk. Something of that sort. But how are you going to see all this from the car?"

! ÜBUNG 61

Übung 61: Wie heißt das Simple Past und das Past Participle der folgenden Verben? Setzen Sie ein!

1. shake
2. bleed
3. fight
4. grip
5. hurt

6. drink

Cinderella looked at Carmody with expectation, her eyebrows raised.
"No ideas?" Cinderella asked, and Carmody shook his head "No."
"Really? I don't know how you got where you are, Geoff," she said, sounding truly amazed. "You're lucky your books are as good as they are. For your information, I have binoculars – with night vision, the kind the British army use. One thing I also plan to look for is whether he's wearing a wedding ring or not."
"That might not tell you anything, Cinderella," Carmody warned. "It may be that he's simply not wearing it for polo practice."
"Quite possibly. That's why we're going to follow him home."
"This will be quite a slow process," Carmody said, "if we have to wait for each night of polo practice."
"That would be inefficient, don't you think?" Cinderella said with a bit of sarcasm in her voice. "Naturally, I don't work that way at all. You'll also be taking down the number plates of several of the cars which we decide on and we'll get addresses for them and visit those houses too. We'll look for detached and semi-detached houses as well as cottages and bungalows. We'll just have to see what we come up with."
"How are you going to get addresses for the number plates?"
"Leave that up to me," she answered quickly.
"But I would like to know how," he insisted.
"Leave that up to me," she repeated.
"I'd prefer not to," he replied.
"What you prefer is of no consequence at the moment." Her voice was harsh and there was clearly no room for compromise.
They sat silently in the car.

Übung 62: Welches Wort ist das „schwarze Schaf"?

1. care, mind, nurse, worry
2. judgement, account, decision, choice
3. pollution, inefficient, incompetent, wasteful
4. big-headed, arrogant, big-hearted, conceited
5. prosperous, affluent, fluent, wealthy
6. cry, weep, sob, hiccough
7. calmly, silently, wordlessly, mutely
8. motorway, highway, freeway, driveway

"I expected a bit more professionalism from you," she added, "a bit more brain-power. I need people with their wits about them."
"People?"
"A person," she countered.
"And you don't think I have my wits about me?"
"I think you're still in a fog of alcohol."
"I am not," he answered, more like a child than a best-selling author.
"I'm disappointed to hear that," she frowned.
"The last thing I want to do is disappoint you," Carmody said.
"Then pull yourself together, man."
"What time is the practice?"
"As I said, it begins at 3 o'clock and ends at 5.30."
"We'll be getting there quite early."
"I wasn't sure how quickly I'd be able to get you on your feet. In any case, they'll probably arrive at least half an hour before practice in order to get changed and to have everything, including the horse, prepared. They have to saddle the horse, for example."
"They'll have people to help them."
"No doubt."

Übung 63: Lesen Sie weiter und ersetzen Sie die unterstrichenen Wörter durch das Gegenteil!

ÜBUNG 63 !

Cinderella parked the car (1.) <u>near</u> __________ from the entrance to the car park. Just (2.) <u>after</u> __________ entering the car park, she had covered up the number plates with white paper.

"So, now we (3.) <u>leave</u> __________," she said, as she reached for the binoculars. She looked through them, to the (4.) <u>exit</u> __________ to the clubhouse, and then put them on the handbrake between the two (5.) <u>back</u> __________ seats.

"How many men should we expect?"

"Certainly not (6.) <u>none</u> __________ of the members will show up. There are about 40 regular members and then many (7.) <u>fewer</u> __________ who no longer play but come for the polo matches and the social functions."

They sat in silence but did not have long to wait. Cars began to arrive every few minutes. There were top-of-the-line German and Japanese imports as well as luxury automobiles made in England. Several men drove up in sports cars as well. Some of the men were accompanied by wives or girlfriends, but most turned up alone. All carried duffle bags inside. Cinderella observed them through the binoculars. They all seemed confident, but she was looking for something more, something she couldn't put into words – something she knew she would recognize if or when she saw it.

In the end, several men did arrive for the polo practice session who were just what Cinderella was looking for – and Carmody wrote down the number plate of each car. These men almost danced out of their cars; they were little bundles of energy – none of them was much over a metre and a half. One young man lit a cigarette and leaned against his car carelessly. Cinderella observed him closely with the binoculars.

! ÜBUNG 64

Übung 64: Setzen Sie die Wörter in die richtige Reihenfolge und bilden Sie sinnvolle Sätze!

1. fast Cinderella drives always.

....

2. wet southern often weather in is England the.

....

3. you your certain plan must be starting before of

....

4. the men their they get watched out of cars

....

5. a person a lot says about the drives who car it

....

6. telephone recognized her he the voice on

....

"A top of the line Mercedes-Benz," she said. "Not exactly subtle

but it's a classic." The car was dark blue, the darkness of the morning sky before the sun has risen. Though by no means small, it was one of the smaller automobiles in the car park.
"Now, he's your type," said Carmody.
"So much for your skills as an observer," Cinderella responded, coolly. "He's not the type for anyone. *You* may see angel wings, but I see a man who thinks he is the modern Adam. Mummy and Daddy gave him everything – and he was lucky enough to inherit good looks as well. He expects women to look at him – and they do."
"He's probably the kind who laughs loudest at his own jokes."

Übung 65: Welche Gegenteile gehören zusammen?

ÜBUNG 65 !

1. possibly	☐ inattentive
2. classic	☐ commonplace
3. observant	☐ cautiously
4. carelessly	☐ modern
5. confident	☐ certainly
6. luxury	☐ timid

Carmody studied Cinderella observing this young man. Although she was a bit turned off by him, she was also clearly attracted to him. She kept the binoculars steadily focused on him.
"He might be a good candidate," she said. "I can't see that he's wearing a wedding ring."
"He isn't the kind who would wear a ring, even if he were married," Carmody asserted.
Cinderella lowered the binoculars for a moment and looked at Carmody. "Now that's the sort of thing I'm looking to hear from you.

Do you think it's your own feeling of insecurity or is it really something you sense?"
"Let me have the binoculars." Close up, Carmody saw a man probably in his late twenties or early thirties with hair just long enough to get in his eyes. He radiated self-confidence. "He's posing even though he doesn't know he's being observed."

ÜBUNG 66

Übung 66: Lesen Sie weiter und unterstreichen Sie die richtige Variante!

Cinderella (1.) suddenly/immediately turned around and looked out of the (2.) windscreen/back window. Then she looked in the mirrors on the car door. Each movement (3.) moved/rocked the car. Noticing her (4.) panic/upset, Carmody asked,
"What's wrong?"
"Nothing. You just gave me a (5.) fright/nightmare."
"How?"
"I thought (6.) of/for a moment that maybe he *was* just posing (7.) for/by us. What if he were there to distract us?"
"Even so, being here isn't (8.) unlegal/illegal."

She rolled her eyes and opened the window briefly to let in some warm air.
"We don't have to be doing anything illegal in order to find ourselves on the wrong side. We are not from the right class, my dear Carmody. You at least are a best-selling writer. I'm nobody."
"A little insecure, are we?"
"Not at all," she answered, rock-hard. "You know Carmody, I'm beginning to think you really are only capable of making one stupid comment after another. I was really excited to meet you, after

reading most of your books, but as a person you're turning out to be a real disappointment."

Carmody sat in stunned silence a moment.

"You are a first-class thief, Cinderella," he nearly whispered, then put his hand on Cinderella's leg, just above the knee. He gently rubbed his thumb back and forth, almost massaging her knee. To his surprise, she said and did nothing, so he left his hand where it was.

Übung 67: Markieren Sie mit richtig ✔ oder falsch – !

ÜBUNG 67

1. Geoffrey Carmody writes novels about lawyers. ☐
2. Cinderella's real name is Catherine Thomas. ☐
3. Carmody saw Cinderella for the first time in a café. ☐
4. Cinderella made a proposal he dared not refuse. ☐
5. The idea of robbing richer people came from Carmody. ☐
6. Carmody does not know Cinderella's telephone number. ☐
7. Inspector Hudson and Carmody are best of friends. ☐
8. Cinderella has read most of Carmody's books. ☐

No other cars came up for more than half an hour. The two sat silently, Carmody with a heart beating to break all records.

"You're making my leg hot," she said at last, and Carmody removed his hand.

He lay back in his seat and closed his eyes. When he opened them again, it had become noticeably darker outside.

"I needed a kip, I reckon." When no one answered, he looked to his right, but the driver's seat was empty. "How did she manage to get out of the car without waking me?" he asked aloud.

ÜBUNG 68 !

Übung 68: Lesen Sie weiter und fügen Sie jeweils die passenden Begriffe in die entsprechenden Lücken ein!
(visible, slipped, ready, escape, managed, spotted, nervous, flicked)

Carmody picked up the binoculars, (1.) ____________ the night vision switch, and turned towards the parked cars. At first he could not find her, but after a few minutes he saw her looking into one of the cars. It was pure luck that he had even (2.) ____________ her, because only the very top part of her head was (3.) ____________. She was right outside the car the young man had been leaning against while smoking. Carmody saw the passenger door open ever so slightly, and she must have (4.) ____________ into the car like smoke. He was wide awake now. With Cinderella in the car, he now kept (5.) ____________ guard over the entrance. He reached for the keys, to be (6.) ____________ to start the car immediately should anything go wrong, but discovered that Cinderella had taken the keys with her. Well, he thought, I'll just have to (7.) ____________ on foot if anything happens. Get out and run into the forest as quickly as possible. Several minutes later, however, he saw her moving back towards the car and keeping close to the ground. She (8.) ____________ to get back in the car almost without opening the door. Immediately she saw that Carmody was awake.

"I'm glad to see you're not sleeping anymore," she said, pulling the door shut so quietly that Carmody almost did not hear it. "Here, take this," she said. He felt a roll of paper in his hand.

"What is it?"

"What is it?" They looked at each other. "Hold it up. There's enough light to see what you've got in your hand."

Carmody did as he was told and saw he was holding a roll of £100 notes in his hand.

Cinderella put the keys in the ignition, started the car and they drove away slowly. She did not turn on the headlights until they were out of the car park.

"I thought we were going to wait and follow one of them home."

"There's been a small change of plan. We're going to wait somewhere else, just in case the police get a phone call."

Übung 69: Welche Wörter passen zusammen?

ÜBUNG 69 !

1. look for	☐	read
2. look after	☐	explore
3. look into	☐	care for
4. look over	☐	investigate
5. look about	☐	search for
6. look on	☐	observe

A little over a kilometre away she found what she was looking for and stopped the car.

"Get out and see if you can help me back the car into the bushes."

"What?"

"Just do it, Carmody. Get out!" Carmody got out and lifted the branch of a tree so that Cinderella could back the car into a hiding place.

"Take the paper off the back number plate," she added. "Perfect," she said, once they were settled. "I can see the road clearly from here."
It was nearly 6 o'clock and getting dark. Carmody expected to hear the sound of police cars racing towards the club at any moment.

ÜBUNG 70 !

Übung 70: Beantworten Sie die Fragen zum Text!

1. What emotion does Cinderella attach to Carmody?

2. What words best describe the men who get out of the cars at the polo stadium?

3. What piece of jewellery does Carmody suggest looking for on the men?

4. Is Carmody jealous of the men they are observing?

5. What was Carmody doing while Cinderella robbed the car?

6. What piece of equipment is quite useful for them?

"Count the money," Cinderella said.
Carmody counted it twice, silently, and then said, "£3200."

“Take your half,” she said.
“No, I did nothing to get this money. All I did was take a nap. It’s all yours. You, er, earned it.”
“We’re partners, Carmody, now take your £1600 and be done with it.”
He opened the glove compartment and put the entire roll of money inside.
It was almost 7 o’clock when they saw the first cars leaving the polo club coming down the road. Quite a few cars went by before they spotted the one they were looking for.
“Get out,” Cinderella said, as she saw it approaching.

Übung 71: Wie heißt das Wort auf Deutsch?

1. binoculars	☐ Schläfchen
2. spot	☐ Ast
3. branch	☐ Abfall
4. nap	☐ Fernglas
5. rubbish	☐ sehen
6. whisper	☐ flüstern

This time Carmody jumped out immediately, and as soon as the car went past he lifted up the tree limb and Cinderella drove out onto the road. Once Carmody was back in, Cinderella drove off at top speed to catch up with the other car. In no time they were behind their target. They followed him onto the motorway and joined the traffic. The driver immediately got into the passing lane and went far over the speed limit. Cinderella did the same but kept a short distance behind. Occasionally other cars pulled between Cinderella’s car and the Mercedes, but Cinderella never lost sight of the car in front.

Übung 72: Setzen Sie das Verb in der korrekten Form ein!

1. Carmody and Cinderella (follow) ________________ a young man from the polo club at the moment.

2. They (work) ________________ together since the beginning of December.

3. Cinderella (believe) ________________ she can control Carmody.

4. The two (have) ________________ a difficult relationship from the beginning.

5. Carmody (never break) ________________ the law before he met Cinderella.

6. Carmody (live) ________________ quietly when Cinderella (come) ________________ into his life.

"It would be amusing if we both got a speeding ticket," Carmody said, "if the police pulled us both to the side of the road, considering we have £3200 of his money sitting in the car."
"Bloody hilarious," said Cinderella, sarcastically.
"We could even pay the fine with some of his money."
"Maybe you could shut up and keep your eye on the car we're following?"
As traffic got heavier, the Mercedes driver was forced to slow down. They finally exited the motorway together and followed him several kilometres away from the motorway into an exclusive neighbourhood.

Übung 73: Haben die Wörter dieselbe Bedeutung? Markieren Sie richtig ✔ oder falsch –!

ÜBUNG 73 !

1. difficult/heavy ☐
2. sight/view ☐
3. chef/boss ☐
4. humorous/amusing ☐
5. dual carriageway/motorway ☐
6. entertainment/hilarious ☐

"Now this is what I was hoping for," Cinderella said, her voice warming up. "Is he going to turn there? No, he's going further, past some very nice places. Now when he stops, Carmody, if he stops on your side of the street, we need the house number and you have to examine the place as best you can and tell me what kind of place it is, how big it is and so forth. If he stops on my side, I need you to try and help me."

At last the Mercedes did turn off and up a curving, U-shaped drive. A detached house set back from the street. It looked as if it had been built in the 1920s. It's boxy shape had perhaps been influenced by the American architect Frank Lloyd Wright.

"House number?" Cinderella asked.

"I'm looking – I'm looking," Carmody answered.

"Did you get it?" she asked impatiently.

"Yes. I'm writing it down."

Übung 74: Lesen Sie weiter und fügen Sie die richtigen Präpositionen ein!

ÜBUNG 74 !

Cinderella drove slowly past, turned (1.) _____ the next street and parked the car (2.) _____ the side (3.) _____ the road.

"What are we stopping (4.) ______?"

"I'm going back (5.) ________ a closer look (6.) ________ the house.

On foot. You stay here with the car."

"This time, leave the keys, please."

"Out of the question," she said, turning the car off and putting the keys in a pocket.

"Then I'm coming with you."

"As you like. But if for any reason we should have to run, you'd better be able to keep up with me."

"Don't you worry about that," Carmody laughed. "Your little trick at the house you robbed forced me to run off, so I know what I can do."

The street was empty, and most of the houses were brightly lit. Some had Christmas decorations in the windows, but most were set too far back from the street for the decorations to be seen very well at night.

"Were you a pretty girl at school?"

"Why would you ask such a question?"

"I'm just trying to imagine what you looked like when you were a girl."

"Do you like little girls?"

"Cinderella – can you be nice to me just once today?"

"No. Now keep quiet."

ÜBUNG 75 !

Übung 75: Lesen Sie weiter und unterstreichen Sie die neun falsch geschriebenen Wörter! Geben Sie die richtige Schreibweise an!

They walked up to the horse openly, as if they were invated guests, and then, after a quick glance aroun, slipped into the shadows and begin to walk around the house. A sign warned that the house had a securaty system. Though they had seen the man dive up to his house, there were very few lights on inside. On the ground floor there was only one light on – perhaps in the kitchen. Because she was too shot to see in the windows, Cinderella told Carmody to put her on his shoulders, so he neeled in front of her. Standing up with her on his shoulders was quite dificult at first.

1. ______________________
2. ______________________
3. ______________________
4. ______________________
5. ______________________
6. ______________________
7. ______________________
8. ______________________
9. ______________________

Though Cinderella was neither big nor heavy, he was not very strong. He managed to hold her steady after a moment and then walked up to a window. At that moment they must have triggered a motion sensor, for a light shone on them in the garden. Carmody ran as well as he could into the darkness. Cinderella held herself up on a tree, taking some of her weight off Carmody's shoulders. Nobody came to the window and eventually the light went off. Carmody then walked over to another window as directed by Cinderella. A little ray of light from another room partially lit the room she was looking in.

"What can you see?" Carmody whispered.

"It's not important," she answered, "I just want to get a feel for the place."

Übung 76: Lesen Sie weiter und unterstreichen Sie die englische Übersetzung der folgenden Wörter!
(heulen, endlich, einsam, zustimmen, schweigsam, Gegend, ängstlich)

Finally she got down from Carmody's shoulders and then said, "Okay, there's one last thing that I always do. I always check for dogs."
"How are you going to do that?"
Without waiting to answer, Cinderella began to wail like a lonesome dog. Other dogs in the area began to answer, but it was silent in the big house next to them.
Carmody, waiting nervously at her side, said, "We should go."
"Okay, let's go," she agreed at last.

Back in the car, Cinderella drove away slowly, as if she were trying to remember everything she could about the location. Then she got back on the motorway and turned the car towards Carmody's far more modest house.
"How are you going to handle the security system?"
"Don't worry, I know what to do."
"I believe that, but I want to know how you are going to disarm it."
"That's a trade secret, Geoff. You never have to deal with that in your books since your stories are always set in the 1920s."
Cinderella parked the car a short distance from Carmody's house, and he invited her in for a drink.
"I'm not interested in seeing you drunk," she warned. "I don't find that a turn-on at all."
"Don't worry, Cinderella. I'll be on my best behaviour, or almost," Carmody answered.

Übung 77: Formulieren Sie die Sätze im Passiv!

1. Cinderella stole the money.

2. The victim did not call the police.

3. Carmody did not drive the car.

4. The author worked on the novel during the day.

5. She was driving the car in the rain.

6. The police have warned him.

She reached over to the glove compartment and retrieved the money. "Here," she said, counting out £1600.
"I've no right to it," Carmody answered. "I didn't help you get it."
"We're partners, remember?"
"I'd prefer not to," Carmody continued.
"Do I need to remind you, Geoff, that one little phone call is all it would take?"
"You just stole £3200 and then threaten me?"
"You sat in the car, Geoff, while I did it. And you sat there with me and observed our potential victims, too."

ÜBUNG 78 !

Übung 78: Übersetzen Sie die Begriffe und enträtseln Sie das Lösungswort!

1. Leber _ _ ☐ _ _
2. Zunge _ ☐ _ _ _ _
3. Magen _ _ _ ☐ _ _ _
4. Nieren _ ☐ _ _ _ _ _
5. Hals _ _ _ _ _ ☐

Lösung: (If you drink too much alcohol you may) _ _ _ _ _

Carmody let her into his house. She walked immediately into the living room and put "his share" of the money on the bar. A couple of minutes later, he joined her in the living room with a bottle of red wine.
"You have a well-stocked wine cellar."
"Why didn't you rob me?" he asked her, while reaching into a china cupboard for some red wine goblets.
"I thought about it, especially after reading your last novel, but then I decided it would be more interesting to work with you."
Carmody handed her a glass of wine, lifted his and said,
"A toast to your beauty."
"To our teamwork," she corrected. Their glasses touched and made a quiet ringing sound.

ÜBUNG 79 !

Übung 79: Welches Wort ist das „schwarze Schaf"?

1. stake, share, steak, portion
2. think, mean, consider, believe
3. contrastingly, additionally, moreover, furthermore
4. intimate, threaten, warn, intimidate

5. dusk, sunset, dawn, evening
6. quaff, drink, guzzle, fizzle

They talked quietly about the evening, especially about the other men who they would investigate. After one glass of wine, however, Cinderella got up to leave.
"Have another glass of wine," Carmody begged.
"I can't. I have to go now."
"You can't leave now, Cinderella. Stay here for a bit longer."
"The name is Cornelia, and I have to leave."
"Neely, stay with me – stay with me tonight." He wanted to make it a sexy appeal, but it sounded pathetic instead.
"Maybe some other time," she answered.
"There's another man waiting for you, isn't there?"
"No, I simply have some things to do."
"Stay with me tonight. You will – "
"I can't. I have my reasons. I'll be in touch."

Übung 80: Markieren Sie mit richtig ✔ oder falsch – !

ÜBUNG 80 !

1. Cinderella gives Carmody £1200. ☐
2. Carmody is happy to have the money and begins planning just how he is going to spend it. ☐
3. Cinderella discourages Carmody from flirting – unsuccessfully. ☐
4. Running alongside Cinderella is no problem for Carmody – or so he thinks. ☐
5. Cinderella always keeps the car keys with her. ☐
6. Outside a potential victim's house, Carmody meows. ☐

She walked towards the door, and Carmody followed her. As she was reaching her hand towards the doorknob, he put his hand on her shoulder and stopped her. He squeezed her shoulder gently but said nothing. Cinderella turned around and looked at him with a quick smile. Carmody leaned forward to kiss her and she turned her lips to him and then quickly pulled away. Suddenly the door was open and she was gone. In the distance he saw Cinderella, walking quickly towards her car parked just around the corner. Carmody suddenly realised the neighbours could see him, so he closed the door and walked back into the living room. He drank up his glass of wine and poured himself another.

! ÜBUNG 81

*Übung 81: Setzen Sie **much** oder **some, many** oder **few** ein!*

1. He does not have ____________ friends.
2. Would you like ____________ wine?
3. I don't have ____________ money with me at the moment.
4. I would like ____________ dressing on my salad.
5. I have a ____________ pounds in the bank.
6. Take ____________ cake home with you, dear.

The following three days, Carmody and Cinderella investigated the other three potential candidates for their robbery. Each day, they arrived at the house before dawn. They sat in Cinderella's car and observed the house. There were long silences, times when Carmody kipped a little, times when Cinderella closed her eyes too. They also talked a bit, but the conversation never got really person-

al. Most of the time Carmody answered Cinderella's questions while his questions went unanswered.
Though Carmody asked several times, Cinderella refused to explain how she had got the addresses for the houses. All she had had were the number plates and from that she had somehow obtained addresses. Carmody asked the question many different ways, suggested numerous ways in which she might logically have got hold of the addresses, but Cinderella revealed nothing. She finally became annoyed with the questioning and told Carmody that if he didn't stop trying to get information from her he would be walking home.

Übung 82: Welche Wörter sind Synonyme?

1. different	☐ tenderly
2. chat	☐ respond
3. answer	☐ diverse
4. potential	☐ banter
5. pathetic	☐ wretched
6. gently	☐ prospective

The first house had white marble columns outside and dated back to the 1880s or 1890s. It was a lovely house with many valuables inside, no doubt. The member of the polo club left around 9 a.m. Just before noon, they watched a woman park her minivan in front of the house and let herself in. A few minutes later, she walked out leading a small army of small dogs of various breeds. About 45 minutes later, she returned and soon afterwards the minivan was gone. Later in the afternoon, a lorry stopped in front of the house, and it looked as if fresh vegetables were being delivered.
The second house was further outside London and the area was

much more affluent than the other two neighbourhoods had been. Cinderella walked up to the house and looked inside through the windows. She discovered that there was at least one servant and theorized that there must be more. The club member left the house at precisely 7.30 am. Forty-five minutes later, they saw a woman with three children leave the house.

ÜBUNG 83 !

Übung 83: Setzen Sie ein sinnvolles Synonym ein!

"Have you seen anything in the newspapers about your (1. theft) r__________?"

"No. I looked for a few days, but then I stopped. I left behind no (2. signs) t__________ – or only yours. Nobody will track the robbery back to you, unless I do something – which is (3. doubtful) u__________." She smiled quickly.

Half an hour later, the woman returned and remained at the house until the middle of the afternoon. "I don't like it," Cinderella said, as they drove away. "No doubt they have plenty of money, but it's too (4. complex) c__________, too many factors –"

"Too many people?"

"Exactly."

The (5. last) f__________ house they observed was more like the first one. The (6. proprietor) o__________ was moderately rich. A maid came at around 8.30 a.m. and soon afterwards was left alone.

Early in the afternoon, the maid left and was replaced, shortly thereafter, by someone who entered with two bags of (7. provisions) f________.

"Very soon, our hero will be home and we can leave, right?"

Cinderella gave Carmody a weary smile.
"Perhaps."
"Look, Cinderella, a joke is a joke. There's not going to be any robbery. Let's go home, drink a bottle of wine and get nice and comfortable. I've got a silk robe that will look lovely on you."
Her eyes got big for a moment. "This is no joke, and I'm rather surprised to hear you say it is." She spoke in such a way that he knew it was best to say nothing further.
"Okay," Cinderella said, "as they drove away from the third house, "we need to look a little closer at our friend in the blue Mercedes Benz."
"I knew you were going to say that. We've just been wasting our time the last three days."
"You have had me all to yourself the whole time," Cinderella smiled. "Doesn't that count for anything?"
"A lot of good it has done me," he snapped.
"What more do you want?" Carmody said nothing. "Besides, as you're now learning, if you want to be a good thief you have to do your homework. Sometimes opportunity knocks, as it did that night at the polo club – and we got a nice sum. Usually, though, you have to prepare yourself and plan every step. Now, we're going to look a little closer at our friend's place. By the way, his name is Foster Wellingborough."
"What?" Carmody asked, astonished. "How do you know his name?"

ÜBUNG 84

Übung 84: Setzen Sie die Sätze in indirekte Rede!

1. I am having a good time.

She/he said (s)he was having a good time.

2. I love good ice cream.

3. I had that for lunch yesterday.

4. I was worried about that yesterday, but I am not anymore.

5. I have been there several times.

6. If you want me, I'll be in the garden.

He looked at her but saw an expression cross her face he had already seen many times. "I know, I know – it's a trade secret."
"Exactly. As I was saying, if our friend leaves over £3000 just sitting around in his car, we should be able to make sure that no one comes into his house on Thursday afternoons; so that while he's having his arm or leg broken we have plenty of time to search his house for his ready money and safe."
"Why Thursday afternoons?"
"Their next practice is not tomorrow but a week from tomorrow. So, we're going to make sure that everything is as I suspect it to be."
"I don't believe you really need my help for that."

"You're right. But I enjoy your company, Geoff. You're such a pleasant person to have around."

Übung 85: Unterstreichen Sie die richtige Variante!

Carmody wasn't (1.) certain/curtain just how ironic she was being, but he wanted to (2.) hope/believe that there was some truth to the (3.) state/statement.
"So, we'll (4.) meet us/meet in the afternoon? Around 2 o'clock or (5.) perhaps/so?"
"My dear, Geoff, I'm nothing if not (6.) thorough/through. I'll meet you at 5.30 tomorrow morning."
"You're *not* (7.) serious/earnest. We've got up at 5 o'clock for the past three mornings. Isn't that enough?"
"We're not finished," she insisted.
"I was hoping to sleep (8.) in/on, finally. You're a nightmare, Cinderella."
"I'm far worse than that, Geoff," she said – and then smiled (9.) for/at him.

At 5.30 the next morning, she was waiting in her car and Carmody staggered out to the car.
"I can't take these hours, Cinderella."
"You just need a bit of training," she said, pulling into the street. "Have some coffee." She held a silver thermos in her hand.
"I've already had two cups of coffee."
"It doesn't smell as if you were out drinking last night."
"I didn't go out and I didn't drink at home – nothing but healthy London water, straight out of the Thames."
"That explains quite a lot, actually," Cinderella said with a brief laugh.

By 6 o'clock, they were sitting outside Wellingborough's house. It was dark inside. A few lights were on in neighbouring houses, but they were the exception, not the rule."

"Everyone's asleep," Carmody yawned, "even in old Wellingborough's house."

"Exactly. We want to see just how many people are asleep in Foster Wellingborough's house."

"What sort of a name is Foster anyway? Why not name him James or Charles or Nigel or Rodney or Richard or something dignified? Foster. What does his girlfriend call him when they're snogging, 'Fossil'?"

"Actually, it's his mother's maiden name," Cinderella said matter-of-factly.

Carmody lifted his head off the headrest of the seat and said, "You're really unbelievable."

Übung 86: Lesen Sie weiter und unterstreichen Sie die englische Übersetzung der folgenden Wörter!

(Hausangestellte, oben, murrte, Angebot, unwahrscheinlich, Überredungskunst, Selbstmitleid, höhnische Bemerkung)

Just after seven in the morning, they saw a maid walk up to the house. She let herself in and a light went on in the kitchen. Soon afterwards a light went on upstairs as well.

"I expect Wellingborough's getting his breakfast in bed," Carmody grumbled.

"No one has ever brought you breakfast in bed, Geoff?"

"No."

"You have to give something in order to get something."

"Cinderella, you would always have breakfast in bed if you stayed with me."

"That's an attractive offer," she said.
"An offer you're unlikely to take up, I'm afraid."
"Your powers of persuasion are not at their best at the moment," she admitted. "Self-pity works with fourteen-year-old girls but not with a woman nearing thirty."
"Nearing thirty? I thought you were already thirty or even thirty-one."
Cinderella gave Carmody a look that let him know that his gibe had missed its mark.

Übung 87: Setzen Sie die Wörter in die richtige Reihenfolge und bilden Sie sinnvolle Sätze!

ÜBUNG 87

1. day I work every drive to. ____________________

2. Paris has twice to once or she been. ____________________

3. do tell do him to what not. ____________________

4. mean so why you are? ____________________

5. got you something have do to? ____________________

6. darling look you marvellous. ____________________

Half an hour later, Cinderella suggested that Carmody go up and look to see what was going on inside the house. "And look to see if you can tell how expensive the furniture is."
"I doubt he has flea market furniture," Carmody responded.
"Why not? You can come across some valuable antiques if you know where to look and know what you're looking for."
Carmody got out of the car feeling that he knew nothing at all about

the world he had spent the last twenty years writing about so successfully. The success of my books, he said to himself as he walked up to the house, is based on my readers' ignorance of the world described in them. He passed the midnight blue Mercedes and continued walking up to the house, his mind on his failures. As Cinderella had suggested, he went around the side of the house and looked in the window. It was a living room, about thirty metres long and twenty metres wide. Whether the furniture was modern or not, he could not really tell. Well, he thought, it isn't antique. It may be high quality, but I know this isn't from the 19th century or before. None of this is furniture from the 1920s either. He saw nobody at all, no dogs or cats, so he began walking back around the front of the house and was walking half-way down the drive when he heard a male voice call.

ÜBUNG 88 !

Übung 88: Fügen Sie die richtigen Präpositionen ein!

1. I'm tired. I'm going to turn ______.

2. Let's turn ______ the television and watch a football game.

3. She turned ______ her neighbour and asked a question.

4. People who wear clothes too young for them turn me ______.

5. When he is stressed he turns ______ a monster.

6. Take your turn ______ the roulette wheel.

"Can I help you?"
Ripped from the interior dialogue he had been having with himself, Carmody stopped and turned around.

"Did you ring?"
"No, I didn't."
"What do you want then?" Wellingborough began to walk towards him. He stopped and looked inside his car for a moment before continuing towards Carmody.
"Nothing," Carmody said, holding his ground. "I was just walking and noticed that I'd walked up your drive. I was somewhat surprised, as you can imagine. I must have been thinking about something else and didn't notice that I'd walked off the pavement. I'm rather absent-minded sometimes."

Übung 89: Lesen Sie weiter und bilden Sie sinnvolle Wörter aus dem Buchstabenchaos!

Wellingborough was now 1. (thwini) __________ five metres of Carmody. He turned 2. (dorun) __________ to look back at his house, as if to see what might have been of interest to the man and, at the same time, to check that nothing was 3. (oobvisuyl) __________ out of place. When he turned back around, Carmody was still standing motionless on the 4. (rdvei) __________. It looked as if Wellingborough were going to say something, so Carmody turned around and 5. (geban) __________ walking towards the street again. "I'm sorry I disturbed you," he said over his 6. (redluohs) __________. Wellingborough said nothing, just watched the stranger walk away. Back on the 7. (ntvmpaee) __________, Carmody walked past Cinderella's car and kept walking until the house was out of sight. He held his 8. (threab) __________ and counted until 60 – though he had to breathe again by 36. He quickly walked back down the street, looked up at Wellingborough's house, and was relieved to see the empty 9. (nalw) __________. He got inside Cinderella's car and slumped in the seat.

"He saw me," Carmody said after a minute.
"This may come as a surprise, Geoff, but I saw everything." The two sat silently for a while. "Did he recognize you?"
"I don't think so. It's not as if I'm a famous pop star or football player or something of that nature."
"No, but there's a picture of you on the back of some of your novels – a picture that should be updated, by the way."
Carmody looked at Cinderella and shook his head. "I'm out of my depth here."
"You are so right," she said, and gave his hand a squeeze.
"What exactly is it you want me to do? What is my role in all this? Am I just here to help with the planning?"
"That – and you'll do the driving. You'll drive the getaway car."
"I'm not the kind of person who would do well on prison food."
"Then you'd better be a good driver."
They watched Wellingborough get in his car, back it down the drive and onto the street. Carmody sank deep into his seat as Wellingborough began driving towards Cinderella's car.
"You can sit up now," Cinderella said. "He's turned the corner and gone."
"I wonder what he does," Carmody said. He saw that Cinderella was about to speak so he added, "No, I don't really want to know."

Up to that point, he had done nothing illegal. He'd been in the car when Cinderella had stolen the money, but that was the closest he had come to being an accomplice. Everything else, from walking into the house that had been robbed to sitting outside houses in the affluent London suburbs, had involved no intentionally illegal action. It might not have *looked* good, but he had broken no law himself. The £1600 was sitting in a glass in his bar, untouched. He could hear Cinderella's repeated threat going through his head: one phone call, Carmody, that's all it would take. He looked over at her. She was so dark and beautiful and young and lively and all the things that he wished he was and all the things he wanted in a woman. She's the perfect woman for me, he thought, if only she were not a thief.

"I'll give you a ring tomorrow," she said as she stopped the car near Carmody's house. "I reckon you're going to go out and have a few pints tonight?"

"That would be a safe bet, Cinderella."

"You might also think about making sure you're in better shape for next Thursday."

"All I have to do is drive."

"You should always be prepared to do a bit of running." With these words, she pulled the door shut and drove away quickly.

Übung 90: Übersetzen Sie ins Deutsche!

ÜBUNG 90 !

1. on horseback ____________________
2. to ride a horse ____________________
3. horse-shoe ____________________
4. horse-hair ____________________

5. stirrup ____________________

6. saddle ____________________

Cinderella called Carmody a couple of times over the next few days. She always called late in the morning when she could be relatively certain he would be awake and out of bed. The conversation never focused on the project that had brought them together. In fact, they tended to flirt over the phone, though Carmody was the more active player, making suggestions and promises.

Carmody spent most of the days working through the text he had written about his joint venture with Cinderella: updating and expanding it, adding details, giving the material he had a finishing touch. If Cinderella thought my last book was weak, he said to himself, she should be pleased with this one. Maybe so pleased that she'll be a bit more open to me. Of course, she may not like the character based on her. She may think I've been a bit hard on her. But she is a hard woman at times.

ÜBUNG 91

Übung 91: Lesen Sie weiter und setzen Sie die Verben in der richtigen Zeitform ein!

Each morning he (1. wake) ____________ hoping she would call. If she (2. not call) ____________ by noon, he (3. know) ____________ that she was probably not going to call, so he focused his energy on writing. For many people, these love pains (4. be) ____________ an unpleasant distraction; they (5. can) ____________ think of nothing and speak of nothing other than these pains. Carmody, however,

(6. be) ______________ used to working in such circumstances. He (7. often be) ______________ very productive just before or just after a woman left him. This time, it was even easier, because when Cinderella was not around, she (8. become) ______________ a bit unreal, like someone you have met in a dream several times but who (9. do) ______________ not exist in the waking world. She was shadowy and hard to hold onto.

On Tuesday morning, she called him earlier than normal. He answered the phone on the third ring.
"What do you say to seeing me today?" she said.
"Just what you would expect me to say: when? Where?"
"But not: why?"
"Perhaps for you there must be a 'why' but not for me. I'm ready to meet you at the drop of a hat."
"Let's meet for dinner, an early dinner."
"Great idea. Afterwards we'll come back to my place."
"That wasn't exactly my plan."
"What was your plan?"
"You go back to your place and I return to mine."
"That's hardly new or romantic. It's not even fun."
"You know that my work has different hours and is not all fun and games. Have you ever heard of the Bearded Lady?"
"Yes, it's an awful restaurant. The food is terrible, the waiting staff is lazy and unprofessional and the building itself lacks anything remotely interesting. Otherwise it's a top-notch restaurant."
"It should be empty then. Meet me there this afternoon at 5.30."
Without waiting for Carmody's reaction, Cinderella hung up.

ÜBUNG 92 !

Übung 92: Welche ist die richtige Bedeutung der Idiome? Kreuzen Sie die richtige Lösung an!

1. to do something at the drop of a hat
   a) ☐ to do something immediately
   b) ☐ to do something because something else happened
   c) ☐ to do something quickly

2. to have your wits about you
   a) ☐ to have money in your purse
   b) ☐ to be thinking quickly
   c) ☐ to have a group of humourous friends

3. to get back on your feet
   a) ☐ to recover from a serious illness
   b) ☐ to look after yourself
   c) ☐ to stand up for yourself

4. to be absent-minded
   a) ☐ to be ignorant
   b) ☐ to be reading
   c) ☐ to be a daydreamer

5. to snog
   a) ☐ to sneeze
   b) ☐ to kiss someone a lot
   c) ☐ to walk through mud and rain

Precisely at twenty minutes to six, Cinderella entered the restaurant. Carmody was already standing at the bar drinking a pint and chatting with the bartender. As soon as he saw Cinderella, he began

walking over to her. The head waiter began guiding her towards a table and disappeared once he had handed the two of them their menus. A moment later, a waitress came up to them and asked if they wanted to order drinks. Carmody ordered another lager and hastily emptied the pint he had. Cinderella ordered a cup of tea.
As the waitress went up to the bar, Cinderella watched her appreciatively.
"If I were a man, instead of talking to the waiter I would have been chatting *her* up."
"That's bad taste when you're meeting another woman for dinner. But maybe after you leave tonight, I'll take your advice."
"It wasn't advice, Geoff, only an observation. So tell me: what have you been doing with yourself since we last saw each other?"
"State secret. For Queen and country and all that, you know? And you, my dear? What have you been doing?"
"Trade secret."
"I believe we're going to be rather short on conversation tonight. I'd like to think that after spending four days with me, you called because you were beginning to miss me, but I know better. Maybe we should get right to the point."
"I thought you said you didn't need a reason to see me."
"I don't. You're a feast for the eyes in that black dress. It brings out the green in your eyes and the light brown of your skin."
"Thank you. Have you been writing?" she asked and then lifted her tea-cup to her mouth.
Carmody watched the cup reach her lips. Her lower lip was fuller than her upper lip, he noticed. "I never talk about what I'm working on, so I'm simply not going to answer your question."
"So," said Cinderella, changing the topic, "are you ready for Thursday?"
"I reckon the question is whether *you* are ready for Thursday. All I

have to do is drive. You're responsible for seeing that Foster Wellingborough takes a bad fall and then breaking into his house, while I sit in a car. My car or yours?"

"My car. It's faster than yours. You're not thinking of backing out, are you?"

"Not at all. I know, you have only to make one phone call and I'm behind bars. I'm really not the kind of guy who would enjoy such a life. But as far as I'm concerned, we're going to visit a friend of yours on Thursday. Or I'll say I thought it was a friend of yours until you robbed the place."

"There won't be any police to explain that to, Geoff. I've never had any contact with police in connection with a robbery."

"Only parking and speeding violations?"

"Just so. We're going to go in once darkness falls. We'll be parking on another street and entering the house from behind. I have walkie-talkies that we'll use to communicate if and when necessary. Since baby-phones sometimes pick up walkie-talkie transmissions, we'll have to keep communication to a minimum. In short, we'll only communicate in case of an emergency."

"Some of the neighbours have babies?"

"I don't know, but I don't want to risk it."

ÜBUNG 93 !

Übung 93: Lesen Sie weiter und finden Sie die Synonyme für die Wörter in Klammern!

The waitress brought their food, (1. disturbing) i__________ their conversation.

"You (2. to be unaware of) d______k______ if any of them have babies." Carmody said, once the waitress had disappeared. "You

(3. astonish) s__________ me, Cinderella."

"Okay, Geoff. You can stop the (4. cynicism) s__________."

"How long do you plan on being inside?"

"Naturally, I want to be in and out of there as (5. rapidly) q__________ as possible. But it may take as long as an hour. I hope that Wellingborough will at least have to be x-rayed, which should take at least an hour. I 6. (think) i__________ he won't be home until late, perhaps ten or eleven or possibly even midnight, but I want to be out of there by 7 o'clock. I should be able to (7. defuse) d__________ the security system and find my way around in that time."

"I know what you'll probably say, but I'll ask just the same. Who's going to take care of Wellingborough?"
"I'll let you in on a secret. Someone I have worked with in the past is going to be taking the place of a member who's away on holiday. With a little make-up and a bit of distance and a rough sport like polo, the players won't notice that he's not their team-mate."
"Am I going to meet him?"
"I hadn't thought about that. Why? Would you like to?"
"Naturally. I'd like to know everyone I'm working with."
"You don't trust me?"
"I trust you implicitly."
"We'll meet early on Thursday."
"Not at 5.30, I hope."
"No, around midday. I have lots to do tomorrow and then I want to

relax on Thursday morning before we have our rather stressful but profitable afternoon and evening."

"Does it ever bother you? Do you ever feel guilty about stealing from other people?"

"If I did, Geoff, I wouldn't do it, now would I? Besides, I'm not stealing from poor people. If you steal from the poor, you can ruin them. The rich always get their money back."

"Just not from you."

"I'm beginning to really like you, Geoff. You have a way of cutting right through to the facts."

"So, you're – " Carmody began.

"Still not going home with you," she finished. After she had paid, they stood and left the restaurant.

"As bad as ever," Carmody said, standing outside on the street.

"I'll see you on Thursday, at noon. Meet me where I usually park my car. Just look as though you're going for a walk."

"Will do."

Carmody went home and wrote until he fell over, exhausted.

! ÜBUNG 94

Übung 94: Unterstreichen Sie die richtige Variante!

He was waiting, as (1.) ordered/requested, when Cinderella drove (2.) on/up.

"Cornelia Thomas," Carmody said, opening the door. "I'm Geoffrey Carmody, (3.) novelist/journalist." He sat down next to her and looked (4.) foreword/forward.

"Pleased to meet you, Mr Carmody," she said, driving (5.) away/on.

"I want to make one thing (6.) transparent/clear," he said. "I am not sitting (7.) in/within this car, while you are inside Wellingborough's house, unless I have the keys."

Cinderella rolled her eyes. "As you like, Geoff."

"Well, I think I'm rather a fool if I sit in a car without keys."

"You can't leave without me."

"I can but I won't. So, where are we going first?"

"We're going to relax and eat a little something."

"You're not going to take me back to the Bearded Lady, I hope."

Cinderella drove to a crowded pub restaurant in the city centre where no one would remember them. She led Carmody to a table where another young man was already sitting, a half-pint glass of beer in front of him.

"Martin Evers, I'd like you to meet Geoffrey Carmody, crime novelist. You said you wanted to meet our partner, Geoff. Here he is: Martin."

Evers stood and offered his hand to Carmody who shook it warmly, examining the younger man.

"You're to be the horseman?" Carmody asked once they were seated.

"He is," Cinderella answered quickly. "I know it's noisy here, but let's keep our voices down. I hope that's your first one," she said to Evers, nodding towards his beer.

"It is."

"*I* hope you're good on a horse," Carmody said.

"Not to worry," Evers answered.

"He's amazing on a horse," Cinderella explained. "He's been on horses and playing polo all his life."

"I've only been playing polo seriously for the last week," Evers corrected, "but I'm a quick learner."

Carmody and Cinderella each ordered a shandy and food. While waiting, Carmody looked back and forth between the two younger people, trying to decide if they were a couple or not. He decided not to ask directly, as the truth – if they were a couple – would have been too much for him at that moment.

"How long have you two been working together?" he asked at last.
"Trade secret," Cinderella answered, without looking at him.
"I should have known better than to ask."
"Yes, you should have," she said.
"We know each other well enough to work together well," Evers answered.
"So what are we going to do after lunch?" Carmody asked very curiously.
"Martin's going to go and get ready to do his part, and we're going to a hardware store."

As they were leaving their table, a tall man briefly exchanged a smile with Cinderella and walked ahead of the three of them. Outside, Cinderella and Carmody said goodbye to Evers and wished him luck. Carmody, meanwhile, looked all around for the other man, but he had disappeared. Where have I seen him before? he wondered.
Cinderella and Carmody walked towards her car. Cinderella held out the keys to Carmody. "You might as well start driving so you get used to it," she said. "It's got a lot more power than your family car."
"Is it my imagination, or is the number plate different?"
"As I said, Carmody, I'm thorough."
They got in the car and Carmody adjusted the seat and the mirrors and then started the car. "Can you drive with winter gloves on? I mean by that, can you really drive, should it become necessary to escape the police, for instance?"
"Of course," Carmody answered, but he removed the gloves just the same. He pulled smoothly into the traffic and drove away. "So, where to?" he asked.
"We're just going to drive around for a while. Martin's going to call

me on my mobile phone when Wellingborough arrives at the club. Once he calls we'll drive to Wellingborough's house and sit there to make sure nobody is there."

"We could go there now to really be sure no one is there."

"But I don't want the car sitting near his house for too long. People will remember a green sports car. We've already spent one day there and a second might be suspicious. Besides, I need to pop into a hardware store."

"What do you need at a hardware store?"

"Geoff, you ask so many questions."

"That's my nature."

Cinderella saw a hardware store.

"Turn here," she said. When he had parked the car, she told him to wait. "I won't be a minute."

She was gone nearly half an hour. That was to be expected, Carmody said to himself. Whenever anyone says, "I'll be back immediately," they usually mean you'll have to wait. After fifteen minutes, Carmody couldn't decide whether he should simply get out of the car and walk away or walk inside the hardware store. He spent nearly ten minutes trying to decide which step would be the best, so Cinderella was back before he had finally made up his mind.

"That was a damned long minute," he complained.

Cinderella patted him on the hand.

"I had to make sure I got what I wanted."

"And what would that be?"

"A little tool that changes magnetism."

"And how is that helpful?"

"It works wonderfully well with security systems, if you know what you're doing."

"I can hardly wait!" Carmody said ironical.

ÜBUNG 95

Übung 95: Welches Wort ist das „schwarze Schaf"?

1. suspicious, dubious, crafty, dodgy
2. obligatory, necessary, vital, charitably
3. for instance, for example, a case in point, for once
4. splash, vanish, disappear, dissolve
5. dive into, nip into, pop into, dash into
6. from A to Z, through and through, backwards and forwards, back and forth

I'm only the driver, Carmody said to himself.
"You know, Cinderella, we could still stop all this and just go to my place. You could move in and we could live together quite happily. You wouldn't have to rob me because everything that's mine would be yours. One of my books is under consideration by a film studio – I could be very rich or we could be very rich very soon, even without robbing a house tonight. Call up your friend Martin and tell him it's all off."
"That's tempting, but I like the challenge of what I do."
"But what about the risks? It would be a shame for a beautiful woman like you to spend some of the best years of your life, the most beautiful years of your life, in prison."
"But I'm not going to go to prison. It's sweet of you to worry about me, though."
They drove around, put more petrol in the car and then drove around some more until finally Martin called. They then turned the car towards Wellingborough's house. They parked, facing the wrong direction on the street, a short distance away and sat.
"It looks rather empty," Carmody observed, as it began to get dark. "No lights on."
They sat a little longer. Cinderella leaned over and began to kiss

Carmody deeply. She kissed him and moaned, “Geoff,” and kissed him some more. Suddenly, an old woman knocked on the window. Carmody, startled, broke off the kiss and rolled his window down, while Cinderella leaned back.
“Can’t you do that somewhere else, young man?”

Übung 96: Unterstreichen Sie im nächsten Absatz die englische Übersetzung der Wörter in Klammern!
(1. wohin jetzt, 2. Schal/Kopftuch, 3. Fenster, 4. klopfen, 5. Stirn)

Carmody looked from the old woman, a scarf stretched over her head, to Cinderella and back again. The woman turned around and walked back up to her house and went inside. Carmody, still not thinking clearly after the double shock of Cinderella’s kiss and the old woman’s knock on the window, started the car and drove away. He looked at Cinderella and wanted to ask what had come over her. Instead, he simply asked, “Where to now?” the cold sweat burning on his forehead, her kiss still on his lips.
“Turn here – and here.” They went around the corner. “Behind this house is Wellingborough’s, if you can believe it. There’s a small patch of forest between the two. Soon, it’ll be dark enough to go through and enter Wellingborough’s house from behind.”
“I thought dawn was your favourite time for this sort of activity.”
“It is, but sometimes you have to bow to necessity.”
“I suppose your targets have usually been single men, like myself, who were out far too late in the night.” Cinderella did not reply. “I should consider myself lucky, if I weren’t a bit worried about – ”
Cinderella’s mobile phone rang.
“Yes. Yes. What? Did you really? Good job. Get out of there as quickly as you can. See you tonight.” She turned her phone off.

"See you tonight?"
"Yes," she said seriously, "after we're finished here, we're going to meet and divide the swag."
"So, he has taken care of Wellingborough?"
"I should think so. It looks like a broken arm and a separated shoulder. The fall took care of the shoulder and a horse took care of the break."
"I'd prefer not to think about it."
"They're waiting for an ambulance as we speak." Cinderella reached into the storage area behind the seats. "Here's the walkie-talkie. All you have to do is leave it on and the channel open. Do not speak to me on it unless you absolutely have to, you understand? If there's an emergency, then I'll let you know – I'll probably just tell you to drive away."
"I couldn't just leave you there."
"Well, you can't go to prison with me, either. They have separate prisons for men and women, so don't play the hero."
Cinderella pulled a black bag out of the storage area, put on a black knitted hat and smeared thick black cream on her face.
"What's in the bag?"
She dropped the walkie-talkie in the bag. "Torches. Two large, one small." She dropped the new tool in it. "Here we go," she said, getting out of the car. "Don't leave without me, unless I tell you to."

ÜBUNG 97 !

Übung 97: Fügen Sie die richtigen Präpositionen ein!

1. We are going to have to move ______ another city.
2. It's time to move ______. This project is a dead end.
3. Our new neighbours are moving ______ tomorrow.

4. My partner moved ______ after five years of living together.

5. You are so slow. Get a move ______!

Carmody watched her disappear into the night, reflecting on the fact that she had answered two questions thoroughly in the last few hours. He reached for the car keys and touched them with relief. He had expected them to be gone. How can you love someone you don't even trust? he asked himself. He pressed a button on his watch and noticed the time: 5.34 p.m. She wants to be out by 7 o'clock, he said to himself. He was nervous, naturally, but suddenly found himself gloomy as well. There in the darkness, all he could do was wait. If I had a character in a book in this situation, I'd be yelling at him to get out of there as fast as he could. Nothing could go right in such a situation. But I can't leave Cinderella. I'll have to leave her tomorrow, tell her tomorrow that I can't live like this, that this isn't the life for me. I can't leave her tonight, though; I can't risk that I would be the one to send her to prison by abandoning her. He also knew that if she were to set her sights on revenge, then she would have her revenge – and no doubt he would be an easy target. Suddenly, Carmody remembered where he had seen the young man at the pub who had smiled at Cinderella. He had been the waiter at the café where he and Cinderella had first gone together.

He looked at his watch. 6.02 p.m. She should be inside and gathering the swag.

What does it mean? he asked himself. Is this person important? What does it mean? Is he her lover? Or her partner? Then who was Martin? How many partners does she have?

It's 6.21 p.m.

"Carmody," the walkie-talkie crackled, "Carmody, I need your

help. I've hurt myself. Come in the back door, on the left side. You should be able to just push it open. Quick. I'm hurt."
"Where are you, Cinderella?" Carmody asked. "Where are you?"

ÜBUNG 98 !

Übung 98: Beantworten Sie die Fragen zum Text!

1. What does Carmody compare his love for Cinderella to?

2. Cinderella worries that Evers has had too much to drink. What is Carmody worried about?

3. Who is to drive the get-away-car?

4. Is Martin Evers their only partner?

5. What injuries does Wellingborough receive?

6. Does Cinderella take the car keys with her into the house?

When he received no answer, Carmody got out of the car, locked it and ran towards Wellingborough's house. He was quickly in the wooded area. He stopped for a moment as a doubt crossed his mind. What if this is a trick? he asked himself. What if it's a trick?

She's done it before – at that first house. But if it isn't a trick, I can't just leave her there. She kissed me. He stood where the trees stopped and looked at Wellingborough's house. The back of the house was clearly a modern addition. All glass, a sun-room to warm and add natural light. No lights were on in the house. He saw the door. It looked closed. The houses to the left and right were lit up. Carmody thought of the waiter again, saw him smile at Cinderella, and then he ran towards the house, bounding up the steps to the door into the sun-room. He gently pushed the door open and walked inside. He glanced around the sun-room and then quickly went into each room on the ground floor. There were four large rooms, including the sun-room – a formal dining and living room, a kitchen large enough for a restaurant, and a large foyer. Old paintings hung on all the walls, except in the foyer, where more modern paintings were hung. There was no sign of Cinderella, so Carmody ran to the stairs and went up to the first floor.

"Cinderella," he called softly. "Cornelia. Neely."

He heard no answer – or else the darkness swallowed the answer. Here on the first floor there were four, five or six doors. One was open and he ran towards it. It was a bedroom and lying on the bed was a bag, but as Carmody ran towards the bed he saw no sign of Cinderella anywhere in the room.

This is a trick, he thought, picking up the thin nylon bag. "If this is a trick," he said out loud, "I'm going to take you down with me." Inside the bag were jewels and a couple of syringes in their original packaging. He ran into hallway with the bag and opened the door to another room – meant to be a library but with only a few books on the shelves. The next room was a sort of office with a large wooden desk and a computer sitting on it. He entered each room and looked around quickly, glanced in all directions, then walked back into the hallway. The next room was another bedroom. One of the windows was open in this room, but not far enough for Cinderella to have crawled through. The window looked out onto the house next door. Carmody lifted the window up and leaned out. Cinderella was not on the ground and it was too steep here for her to have crawled out and made her way down. He pulled his head back inside and turned around. As he walked back to the door, he saw a walkie-talkie lying on the floor. I have got to get out of here, he said to himself. "Cinderella, you ...!" he screamed.

He ran down the stairs. Just over the front doorway, he saw a red light flashing. The alarm must be going off, he thought as he ran towards the back door. He began to hear the sounds of sirens coming closer. He ran to the sunroom, threw open the door, jumped to the bottom of the outdoor steps and ran to the wooded area, then through it and back to the car.

ÜBUNG 99 !

Übung 99: Setzen Sie die Sätze in indirekte Rede!

1. You can drive.

2. I fell down and hurt myself.

3. Wait for me in the car!

4. I'll be back in a moment.

5. I have worked with Martin Evers for three years.

6. Where do you go at Christmas time?

"It's gone," he said, suddenly feeling dizzy. Cinderella's green sports car was gone. "She left *me* here." The bag dropped from his hand. The sirens were coming ever closer. What do I do now? Walk away. Walk away quickly but not too quickly. Absent-mindedly, he picked the bag up and began to walk. A first and then a second police car went past at high speed, the sirens screaming. After the second one passed, he realised what he was carrying in his hand and threw the bag into some shrubberies. A third car drove by with its lights on but much slower. The officer in the passenger seat observed Carmody quite closely. The car continued past and Carmody breathed a sigh of relief. He kept walking and didn't notice that the police car had stopped. There was a sound of squealing tyres and suddenly the police car was driving backwards down the road. It stopped and the officers got out and walked towards Carmody.

"There's been a robbery not far from here," one of the police officers said. Carmody could not see either of them very well in the darkness. "May we see some identification?"

"I don't have anything with me," he said, though in fact he did. "I just came out for a walk."

"Do you live around here?"

"Yes," he answered.

"May we take you home?"

"But I'm out for a walk. I don't want to go home yet."

"May we see your keys?" the other officer asked.

Carmody held out his own house keys.

"Someone meeting your description was seen carrying a small bag. What happened to it?"

"As I said, I came out for a walk. I didn't bring anything with me."
"What's your address?"
When Carmody did not answer immediately, one of the officers said, "Okay, let's walk back the way you came," and pulled out a torch and began sweeping the ground with it.

Übung 100: Welche Wörter haben dieselbe Bedeutung?

1. description	☐ bush
2. shrubbery	☐ siren
3. identification	☐ instantly
4. warning	☐ portrayal
5. theft	☐ credentials
6. immediately	☐ burglary

They began to walk, Carmody helplessly sandwiched between the two men. They walked for about two hundred metres when the nylon bag was lit up in the shrubbery. One of the officers leaned over and picked up the bag. He opened it and pulled out a syringe.
"Now that's a nasty habit," he said.
"That's not my bag. I've never seen it before in my life. Besides, I don't even like syringes. I'm scared of them."
"That's a good one," one of the officers answered sarcastically.
"Now, do I look like a drug user?" Carmody asked.
Neither officer answered the question. "There's some jewellery in here as well, but not very much. Where's the rest?" he asked Carmody.
"How should I know? I've never seen the bag before in my life."
"I think you'd better come with us."
"I'd rather just go home."

"Can you tell us your street address?"
Carmody stood there silently. He did not know the address of the house he had spent nearly an hour in front of. "I can direct you there."
"You want me to believe that you just forgot your address?"
"You make me nervous, the two of you, accusing me of being a drug addict and a thief."
"Come with us, please." They led him to the police car and sat him in the back seat.

Übung 101: Welche Antwort passt zur Frage? Kreuzen Sie an!

1. What is Carmody doing at the moment?
   a) ☐ He walks with police officers.
   b) ☐ He has walked with police officers.
   c) ☐ He is walking with police officers.

2. How long have Carmody and Cinderella known each other?
   a) ☐ For about four weeks.
   b) ☐ Since about four weeks.
   c) ☐ They knew each other about four weeks.

3. Where do you live?
   a) ☐ I am living not far from here.
   b) ☐ I am live not far from here.
   c) ☐ I live not far from here.

4. Where is the bag you were carrying?
   a) ☐ I carry not a bag.
   b) ☐ I was not carrying a bag.
   c) ☐ I am not carrying a bag.

5. What are you doing out so late at night?

a) ☐ I am taking a walk.

b) ☐ I take a walk.

c) ☐ I have taken a walk.

Once they were both in the front seat, they drove to Wellingborough's house and parked alongside the other two police cars. The two officers then got out of the car and walked up to the other officers. When they came back, the shorter one asked for Carmody's name.

"Geoffrey Thomas," he answered.

"Your profession, Mr Thomas?"

"Why am I being asked these questions? Am I a suspect?"

"At the moment, everyone is a suspect."

"Even you?"

The officer looked at him and frowned. "Don't be ridiculous."

"What is ridiculous," said Carmody, gathering all his courage, "is that a man can't take a walk in his own neighbourhood without being picked up by the police."

"Tell us your address."

"I'm not going to. I don't want to be taken home by the police. That's just the sort of thing to get neighbours talking, if they should see me getting out of a police car. You have no reason to be holding me."

"We have the bag with jewels and your syringes."

"I already told you, I never saw that bag before in my life. It isn't mine. And as for the syringes, you can check my arms: I have no needle marks at all. I find such a habit as distasteful as you do."

"We're going to take you down to the station and take your fingerprints and then you'll be free to go," said the shorter police officer. "First, however, we will need an address."

Carmody sat quietly while the officers drove to their station. Once there, they handed him over to an assistant who took down his information and took his fingerprints. Carmody gave the same name but this time he provided an old address, not as far from the crime scene as where he currently lived. Before he left, he was allowed to make a call to a friend to give him a lift home.

"Yes, I know. Yes. I know. Well find someone who hasn't been drinking then. Just come here and pick me up, will you?" he yelled into the phone.

Übung 102: Lesen Sie weiter und setzen Sie die Verben in der richtigen Zeitform ein!

Everything (1. go) ________________ wrong in his life in the last few weeks. Ever since he (2. meet) ________________ Cinderella his life (3. simply spiral) ________________ out of control. Now, he (4. know) ________________ that she (5. never be) ________________ interested in him. She had set him up. But, really, he (6. do) ________________ nothing wrong. It (7. not look) ________________ good, but he (8. not do) ________________ anything illegal – except, perhaps, for driving a getaway car.

But he had been left at the house, so he had not even driven the getaway car. Things had turned out quite differently from the way he had planned them. In his story, he and Cinderella were together at the end. He had left it unclear whether she actually committed the robbery or not. He had always hoped that he could talk her out of it.

He had wanted to discover that being a thief was not important for her; it would not be a fundamental change in his eyes. Now it was clear that he had completely underestimated her. Though they had spoken on the phone several times and met a handful of times, he had never really got an insight into the real Cornelia Thomas – or whatever her name was.

When he got home, Carmody thoroughly searched his house for jewels and money, looking for anything that was not his. He searched the house but came up empty. Finally, at 3 o'clock in the morning, exhausted, he lay down in his bed and hoped for a blissful night of sleep.

Bump, bump bump!

Carmody rolled out of bed.

Bump, bump bump!

He pulled a robe on and went downstairs to the front door.

"Who is it?" he called out.

"The police."

! ÜBUNG 103

Übung 103: Lesen Sie weiter und finden Sie jeweils die Synonyme für die Wörter in Klammern!

Carmody opened the door and they walked in. They showed him some (1. documents) p__________, which he did not (2. trouble) b__________ to read, and began to search the house.

"Why didn't you give us your (3. actual) r__________ name and address?" an officer asked. Carmody did not (4. identify) r__________ the officer. When Carmody did not answer, he

(5. went on) c______________: "That was a big (6. blunder) m__________. And what were you doing so far away from central London on foot?" This officer and another asked several more (7. enquiries) q__________ of a similar sort.

"I was up there with my girlfriend," Carmody finally answered. "We had an argument, and she got in her car and drove away."
"What were you doing there? That's not one of the usual romantic areas for lovers. You ever heard of the white cliffs of Dover or the Pennines?"
"I like architecture."
"You like architecture."
"Do you know what happened to Foster Wellingborough?"
"No. Should I?"
"His house was robbed of more than £18,000 cash and several priceless pieces of jewellery *and* he's in hospital."
"I had nothing to do with the robbery, and I certainly didn't do anything to him."
"No, he fell from a horse," the officer said. "Someone posing as a member knocked him off his horse."
"We found your fingerprints inside the house," another officer reported. "On the open window on the first floor. And we found them on jewellery at a Dr Zeno's house. Do you know a Dr Zeno? No? He's a dentist. His house was robbed about three weeks ago while he and his wife were away on holiday. There's a brooch and several other pieces of jewellery with your fingerprints on them."
Carmody turned white and all the spirit of resistance drained out of him. He sat down on his sofa and watched the officers taking his place apart bit by bit.

"You gave us the wrong name, but someone recognized your picture. I reckon you're a little too famous now."

"I would like to speak to Inspector Hudson," he said at last.

"A solicitor might be a better choice," the officer recommended.

"I'm afraid I'm beyond the help of any solicitor."

"I would have to agree," one of the officers said.

The police took him to a larger police station and put him in a cell and there he waited. He had no idea whether he was going to be questioned or whether Cornelia Thomas might just somehow turn up and set him free. That afternoon, he was taken out of his cell twice and put into a police line-up. As he later learned, he was positively identified twice – by Foster Wellingborough's elderly neighbour and by Wellingborough himself.

"The elderly neighbour saw you snogging a 'dark-haired beauty' on the day of the robbery. Is this 'dark-haired beauty' your accomplice?"

"I had no accomplice," Carmody answered, "because I committed no crime."

"Wellingborough couldn't say exactly what day it was, but he saw you walking up to his house several days before the robbery. He too positively identified you yesterday."

"I would like to speak with Inspector James Hudson of Scotland Yard," Carmody answered.

"Are you one of the Inspector's friends? Do you think he can just set you free? You forget, Mr Carmody, we have fingerprints – your fingerprints – *in* Dr Zeno's house and *in* Foster Wellingborough's house. We also have a very interesting story written by the famous Geoffrey Auberon Carmody, wherein a novelist is led astray by a young thief, with long, dark brown hair, named Cinderella. Why don't you give us her real name, tell us where she lives and tell us anything and everything else you know about her and these two robberies. Perhaps you *were* led astray."

"I want to speak to Inspector Hudson," Carmody said, his voice going suddenly weak. How could he have forgotten about the story?! He should have sent it to his agent and then deleted it from his computer; if not his agent, he should have sent it to someone else, his sister perhaps, but to have left it on his computer: how stupid can you be? he thought. The answer of course was quite simple: stupid enough to leave it on his computer.

Übung 104: Fügen Sie die richtigen Präpositionen ein!

The following day a solicitor visited him (1.) ______ his cell. He was a heavy-set pink-cheeked man (2.) ______ his mid-40s, who was familiar (3.) ______ two (4.) ______ Carmody's books. Carmody signed the books placed (5.) ______ the table (6.) ______ front (7.) ______ him; however, he refused to speak to him (8.) ______ the case, beyond saying that he had already told the police everything he knew.

"You're on the express train to jail, you know? I mean," he said loudly, "this is a high-speed train to jail you're on. They have fingerprints inside two different houses and on jewellery that was recovered from both houses. Moreover, you may not know this, but the green sports car the neighbour saw you sitting in with 'Cinderella' – or whatever you wish to call her – turned up abandoned yesterday. It was stolen five weeks ago. Whoever drove it was careful – your fingerprints were still on the steering wheel. They can prove you were driving a stolen vehicle. You clearly had accomplices, but if you cover for them then the only person who is going to suffer is you."

"The only person who can help me," Carmody said emphatically, "is Inspector James Hudson of Scotland Yard."

"I don't think that even he can help you," the solicitor said, shaking his head.

"Thank you for coming, Inspector."

"I don't know what I can do for you, Mr Carmody."

They stood in a large, dark room, with a massive wooden table in the centre. In this room, Carmody had been questioned several times already and as he was being led to the room he was fully expecting yet another round of questions. He had been quite pleased therefore to see Inspector Hudson standing quietly in a corner of the room, his hands in his trouser pockets. Dressed in a dark suit with a bright burgundy shirt, Hudson did not smile as he saw Carmody brought into the room. Carmody on the other hand smiled broadly at the inspector.

"I read your story," Hudson said, once the two men were alone. "It made for some very interesting reading. It should help get you in jail – and then on another best-seller list, if your publisher is smart enough to bring it out. Your description of Dr Zeno's house and the jewellery that you claim you found in your house, or that you took from Dr Zeno's house, was quite accurate. Naturally, the police think that the story is a fictionalised version of your life the last few weeks put on your computer especially for them – as your alibi."

"That story is the truth," Carmody said. "I've never written anything truer."

"In the story, she says she prefers to rob houses at dawn. Why rob Wellingborough at 5.30 at night?"

"Pure necessity."

"And the plan came from you?"
"Yes, but I never meant for it to really happen. The details were all planned and carried out by her."
"I've never really seen you as pathetic, Carmody. And this young woman played a game with you and had you wrapped around her finger, so that you would do anything for her? You want me to believe that? You're usually the aggressive type, aren't you, when it comes to women? At least that's how I remember you."

Übung 105: Unterstreichen Sie die richtige Variante!

ÜBUNG 105 !

Ignoring (1.) that/this last statement, Carmody declared, "I didn't rob (2.) anyone/no-one and you can search my house and my bank accounts and you won't find (3.) nothing/anything (4.) a/n bookholder/accountant can't explain."
"So you've hidden the (5.) treasure/swag somewhere," Hudson suggested. "Simply because they can't (6.) find/found it, does not mean you don't have it."
"You must (7.) remind/remember that I called you about three or four weeks ago and you (8.) lay down/hung up on me. That was the day I found the jewellery in my (9.) building/house."
"You should have called the police (10.) straight on/immediately."

"I called you instead. And soon after that I stopped thinking straight, as you know from the story: I met Cinderella."
"What's her real name?"
"Cornelia Thomas." Carmody watched Hudson pull out a little black notebook, open it and write the name inside.
"I'll look her up immediately," he said, putting his pen and notebook back in his inside pocket.

"There's no point, Inspector. It isn't her real name."

"How do you know?"

"I know."

"But you don't know her real name?"

"No. I don't know much about her at all. I never got a phone number or an address for her. She always made the contact, and I was so happy to talk to her or see her that I didn't dare push for more from her. I think at least one or two men may have worked with her but I don't know for certain." Carmody described his visit to the pub the day of the robbery.

"I admit that I was with her the night of the robbery. I sat in the car that was to help her escape with the swag. I told her she didn't need to steal from people, that she could live with me, but she said 'No.' She said that such a life was not interesting to her. She called me on the walkie-talkie, while I was waiting for her in the car, and said she had been injured. I didn't know what had happened, and even then I suspected it was a trick. Be that as it may, I went in Wellingborough's house and looked for her everywhere. I saw a window open on the first floor, found the bag and then heard the sirens."

"A walkie-talkie was found in Wellingborough's house, but it had no fingerprints on it."

"She set me up. I don't know why, but she did. She got me in the house, got some jewels in my hands and made sure the police were on their way. And the syringes were simply the icing on the cake – to make it look particularly bad."

"You're moving a little fast, Carmody. I'm not sure I believe you were set up." Hudson looked at Carmody with the grim face he reserved for hardened criminals. "And I have to tell you that in any case it doesn't look good. Nobody believes your story. The district attorney thinks your trial should be a rather brief one. He feels there's no need to waste time on a long trial. Even your solicitor told me the best he could do for you was to get a reduced prison term. It doesn't matter whether you were seduced or not. You're still responsible for your own actions."

"But I didn't *do* anything," Carmody said, sinking into his chair. "I was led into the Zenos' house as part of a trap. I went into Wellingborough's house only to save Cinderella. I did not rob either house, and I didn't intend to rob either house. I'm innocent of everything – except being foolish."

"Most of the people in prison could say the same thing," Hudson answered.

"I suppose you're right," Carmody responded, shaking his head. "But she set me up. She said she was not a good planner, but she is a master planner. If anyone can capture her, you can."

"I'll see what I can do," Hudson said, relaxing, "but I'm certain you will be behind bars before I find anything out."

"I can wait," Carmody said.

"I don't see that you have any other choice." Hudson was silent a moment. "But, if there is some truth to your story, you won't be behind bars for long, I can assure you of that. If there is a Cinderella, then it's nearly midnight for her."

Carmody did not look at Hudson very happily.

Abschlusstest

Übung 1: Welches Wort ist das „schwarze Schaf"?

1. think, pond, reflect, consider
2. natural, normal, sensual, usual
3. upset, shocked, surprised, startled
4. directory, list, file, record
5. threaten, intimate, warn, intimidate
6. vanish, dissolve, splash, disappear

Übung 2: Setzen Sie die Verben in die richtige Zeitform!

1. They (know) ____________ each other for a long time.

2. We (work) ____________ on a report at the moment.

3. She always (drive) ____________ like a maniac.

4. Last summer, I (fly) ____________ to Paris.

5. He (live) ____________ in Oxfordshire since 1999.

6. They (talk) ____________ in the kitchen, when the phone (ring) ____________.

Übung 3: Finden Sie das passende Gegenteil!

1. amateur	☐ reluctant
2. strange	☐ important
3. calm	☐ expert

4. willing	☐	nervous
5. inconsequential	☐	artifical
6. natural	☐	ordinary

Übung 4: Fügen Sie die richtigen Präpositionen ein!

1. Will you look ______ this report for me?

2. Punctuality means being _____ time.

3. The mayor is ______ charge ______ running the city.

4. There was no sign ______ our dog anywhere.

5. He turned ______ his wife and asked her the same question.

6. They moved ______ after only two years.

Übung 5: Welche Synonyme gehören zusammen?

1. shattered	☐	proprietor
2. excited	☐	trace
3. limit	☐	wretched
4. exact	☐	exhausted
5. pathetic	☐	papers
6. potential	☐	think
7. sign	☐	real
8. owner	☐	wound up
9. documents	☐	boundary
10. imagine	☐	prospective
11. actual	☐	precise

Übung 6: Wie lauten die Sätze in der richtigen Reihenfolge?

1. one late home morning got he

2. day do have something you to every

3. weekend swimming often go we the at

4. work do how get you to?

5. try will you you hard succeed if

6. Finland been I never to have

Übung 7: Bilden Sie sinnvolle Wörter aus dem Buchstabenchaos!

1. rusesirp
2. fertfo
3. vopelene
4. nithiw
5. tacavnio
6. haedeorf

Übung 8: Setzen Sie die Sätze in indirekte Rede!

1. You are wonderful.

2. Your English has improved quite a bit.

3. You can always stay with me.

4. If you call me, I'll tell you.

5. I was there yesterday.

6. She should always do what she is told.

Übung 9: Welche ist die richtige Bedeutung der Idiome? Kreuzen Sie die richtige Lösung an!

1. to hit it off with someone
   - a) ☐ to look for something in a field
   - b) ☐ to start a venture with someone
   - c) ☐ to have a good relationship with someone

2. to have your wits about you
   - a) ☐ to have money in your purse (not just the bank)
   - b) ☐ to have a group of entertaining friends (not just funny)
   - c) ☐ to be intelligent (not just book knowledge though)

3. to lend someone a hand
   a) ☐ to help someone
   b) ☐ to give someone a place to stay for the night
   c) ☐ to give someone some food

4. to be absent-minded
   a) ☐ to be a daydreamer
   b) ☐ to be reading
   c) ☐ to be unintelligent

5. to rise to the challenge
   a) ☐ to get up with the alarm clock
   b) ☐ to perform well because you have to
   c) ☐ to try and be successful

6. to have a word with someone
   a) ☐ to speak with someone
   b) ☐ to go into a meeting with someone
   c) ☐ to disagree with someone

Übung 10: Markieren Sie mit richtig ✔ oder falsch – !

1. Geoffrey Carmody and Hudson are the best of friends. ☐
2. Cinderella is about 19 years old. ☐
3. A dentist is robbed as the story begins. ☐
4. The other partner is called Martin Springer. ☐
5. Carmody is a writer whose novels deal with crimes. ☐
6. A green sports car was stolen. ☐
7. Cinderella drives off to a store, leaving Carmody behind. ☐
8. Carmody is arrested. ☐

Lösungen

Übung 1: 1. awoke 2. was 3. ached/was aching 4. convinced 5. swallowed 6. decided 7. met 8. froze

Übung 2: 1. mind 2. afternoon 3. ferocious 4. exhibitionist 5. open 6. pond

Übung 3: 1. materialise/disappear 2. expert/amateur 3. ornate/plain 4. common/unusual 5. expected/bewildering 6. previous/next

Übung 4: 1. in 2. of 3. at 4. in 5. of 6. to 7. in

Übung 5: 1. insult 2. impolite 3. unbekannt/nicht identifiziert 4. suit 5. ernstlich 6. reasonable

Übung 6: 1. surprised 2. doorbell 3. letter 4. effort 5. envelope 6. frowned

Übung 7: 1. leaves 2. bough 3. stem 4. tree trunk 5. blossoms 6. thorns, Lösung: autumn

Übung 8: 1. He wrote very simple stories. 2. He got home late one morning. 3. What does that word mean? 4. He was already on the train. 5. A woman took all her clothes off. 6. Cinderella is a beautiful young woman.

Übung 9: 1. silents (silence) 2. chamdelier (chandelier) 3. corridoor (corridor) 4. dout (doubt) 5. intereor (interior) 6. sported (spotted) 7. stomache (stomach) 8. luxurusly (luxuriously) 9. antiq (antique) 10. pilow (pillow)

Übung 10: 1. He writes crime novels. 2. He sees a dress. 3. The dress is black. 4. It is a nature picture – with a branch and blossoms on it. 5. The shoe reminds him of a cat. 6. The shoe reminds him of the character Cinderella.

Übung 11: 1. richtig 2. falsch 3. richtig 4. richtig 5. falsch 6. richtig

Übung 12: 1. Ente 2. Adler 3. Schlange 4. Eule 5. Esel 6. Eichhörnchen 7. Maultier/Maulesel 8. Fledermaus

Übung 13: 1. later/afterwards 2. tired/shattered 3. wound up/excited 4. notice/observe 5. opposite/across from 6. taking a deep breath/plunging in

Übung 14: 1. cut 2. bought 3. sought 4. could 5. wore 6. stood

Übung 15: 1. fetch 2. handed 3. smile 4. tone 5. real 6. dawn

Übung 16: 1. important/minor 2. favourite/detested 3. encourage/deter

4. contrast/likeness 5. hard/easy 6. nervous/calm 7. comfortable/prickly 8. slender/stout

Übung 17: 1. sound 2. trophy 3. consumption 4. politician 5. sensual 6. pub

Übung 18: 1. telling **to** me 2. believe **in** his ears 3. **the** Cinderella 4. **slow** reaction 5. **percentage** profits 6. very **the** least 7. burglaries **not** only 8. are **to** some 9. **the** burglary 10. its **for** entertainment

Übung 19: 1. call 2. stick 3. like 4. deliberation 5. postpone 6. along

Übung 20: 1. It might be Cornelia Thomas. 2. Yes, she did. 3. Yes, he did. 4. No, he is not. (It took him 30 minutes to recover from his run.) 5. She is in her late twenties. 6. Her favourite time to rob a house is at dawn.

Übung 21: 1. He always read the newspapers. 2. She preferred to rob houses at dawn. 3. Cinderella sent Carmody a postcard. 4. People worry about getting older. 5. How do you catch a thief? 6. It might be a good career move.

Übung 22: 1. discuss 2. So 3. almost 4. league 5. challenge 6. target 7. into 8. somewhat 9. whisper

Übung 23: 1. aid 2. precise 3. delightful 4. boundary 5. talk about 6. most recent

Übung 24: 1. banch (bench) 2. painted (pointed) 3. through (though) 4. prefered (preferred) 5. uper (upper) 6. carlessly (carelessly) 7. parterre (partner) 8. risiko (risk)

Übung 25: 1. jealous 2. partnership 3. throat 4. challenge 5. life 6. modern

Übung 26: 1. Zahnarzt/dentist 2. Schweiz/Switzerland 3. Vorschlag/suggestion 4. Lösung/solution 5. Zäune/fences 6. Forschung/research 7. Firmen/companies 8. Diener/servants

Übung 27: 1. thieves 2. journeys 3. wives 4. children 5. bodies 6. novels 7. leaves 8. feet

Übung 28: 1. c 2. a 3. c 4. b 5. a 6. c

Übung 29: 1. richer/richest 2. better/best 3. worse/worst 4. more expensive/most expensive 5. more/most 6. prettier/prettiest

Übung 30: 1. falsch 2. falsch 3. richtig 4. richtig 5. falsch 6. richtig

Übung 31: 1. satisfactory 2. probation 3. upset 4. time 5. preserve 6. run onto
Übung 32: 1. in 2. in/of 3. on 4. for 5. in/of 6. on
Übung 33: 1. cosy/comfortable 2. leisure/pleasure 3. hurry/rush 4. demanding/hard 5. fancy/prefer 6. slight/bit of a
Übung 34: 1. How 2. Where 3. What 4. Why 5. Which 6. When
Übung 35: 1. silent 2. questions 3. distance 4. location 5. observe 6. really 7. towards
Übung 36: 1. membership fees 2. club members 3. seat belt 4. tube station 5. sit down 6. practical joke
Übung 37: 1. friendly 2. open 3. explosion 4. step 5. step 6. reckon 7. suitable 8. right 9. leave
Übung 38: 1. c 2. b 3. b 4. a 5. c
Übung 39: 1. How do you get from point A to point B? 2. She drives a bright green sports car. 3. We leave on Thursday at 9 a.m. 4. If I were you, I would accept the job/I would accept the job if I were you. 5. You should do this anonymously. 6. How often do you visit London?
Übung 40: 1. falsch 2. falsch 3. richtig 4. falsch 5. falsch 6. richtig
Übung 41: 1. guide 2. specialising 3. chose 4. youth 5. up 6. correctly 7. old 8. basic 9. stars
Übung 42: 1. imediately (immediately) 2. reserch (research) 3. prodused (produced) 4. royally (royalty) 5. wandered (wondered) 6. provided (provid-ed) 7. struktur (structure) 8. representatatives (representatives) 9. excited (existed) 10. completed (competed)
Übung 43: 1. The car was driven by Cinderella. 2. All (the) decisions were made by Cinderella. 3. The painting was stolen (by someone). 4. This product was made (by workers) in China. 5. Responsibility for the crime was taken by an anonymous group. 6. Baked beans are eaten by the British a lot.
Übung 44: 1. badly 2. artificial 3. ignorance 4. peasants 5. previous 6. latter
Übung 45: 1. pounded/knocked 2. organizer/filing cabinet 3. moment/time 4. alongside/next to 5. newest/latest 6. looked/appeared 7. begin/launch into 8. short/brief 9. advantages/benefits 10. grudgingly/unwillingly

Übung 46: 1. progress 2. laughed 3. joke 4. members 5. spring 6. rates

Übung 47: 1. teilnehmen 2. selbstsicher 3. Fortschritt 4. streng 5. Gipfel 6. Nachteil

Übung 48: 1. courage 2. brake 3. cabinet 4. handy 5. file 6. do

Übung 49: 1. Geoffrey Carmody always writes on his computer. 2. He drives to work every day. 3. She works full-time as a thief. 4. We were in Manchester last month/We went to Manchester last month. 5. Carmody has won many awards. 6. They need new uniforms immediately.

Übung 50: 1. He does not want the assistant manager to recognize him. 2. He says he works for *Three Kings*. 3. No, she does not. 4. He almost calls him "Tommy." 5. Yes, indeed he is. 6. (A trick question!) He cannot contact Cinderella – he has no phone number or address for her.

Übung 51: 1. sound 2. tell 3. whole 4. concluded 5. worry 6. events

Übung 52: 1. endure 2. embellish 3. exactly 4. including 5. kitten 6. dedicate 7. remove

Übung 53: 1. richtig 2. richtig 3. falsch 4. falsch 5. falsch 6. richtig 7. falsch

Übung 54: 1. It was now about 3.15 p.m. 2. I was searching for sunken treasure. 3. And you bought a swim-suit and a swimming pool as a Christmas present. 4. Maybe I'll tape my Christmas cards up on the walls, he thought. 5. I should take a walk, down on the beach at the Prince of Wales' castle.

Übung 55: 1. to 2. of 3. for 4. of 5. to 6. in 7. for 8. of 9. onto

Übung 56: 1. a secret 2. stinks 3. partners 4. you suffocate 5. invades 6. champagne 7. curtains

Übung 57: 1. abbiegen, werden 2. ausruhen, lehnen 3. anrufen, nennen 4. klein, kurz 5. Kiste, Brustkasten 6. erreichen, ausstrecken

Übung 58: 1. boil 2. pot 3. cupboards 4. for 5. tough 6. around 7. harshly 8. after

Übung 59: 1. for 2. since 3. for 4. since 5. since 6. for

Übung 60: 1. Doran is not allowed to give the list to people outside the company. 2. She tells him on the phone. 3. He drinks a lot of alcohol. 4. A glass of water. 5. He opens a can of baked beans. 6. She certainly does not admire his cooking.

Übung 61: 1. shook, shaken 2. bled, bled 3. fought, fought 4. gripped, gripped 5. hurt, hurt 6. drank, drunk

Übung 62: 1. nurse 2. account 3. pollution 4. big-hearted 5. fluent 6. hiccough 7. calmly 8. driveway

Übung 63: 1. away 2. before 3. wait 4. entrance 5. front 6. all 7. more

Übung 64: 1. Cinderella always drives fast. 2. The weather is often wet in southern England. 3. You must be certain of your plan before starting. 4. They watched the men get out of their cars. 5. A car says a lot about the person who drives it. 6. He recognized her voice on the telephone.

Übung 65: 1. certainly 2. modern 3. inattentive 4. cautiously 5. timid 6. commonplace

Übung 66: 1. suddenly 2. back window 3. rocked 4. panic 5. fright 6. for 7. for 8. illegal

Übung 67: 1. falsch 2. falsch 3. falsch 4. richtig 5. falsch 6. richtig 7. falsch 8. richtig

Übung 68: 1. flicked 2. spotted 3. visible 4. slipped 5. nervous 6. ready 7. escape 8. managed

Übung 69: 1. search for 2. care for 3. investigate 4. read 5. explore 6. observe

Übung 70: 1. disappointment 2. confident, energetic 3. a wedding ring 4. Yes, he is. 5. He was sleeping. 6. binoculars with night vision

Übung 71: 1. Fernglas 2. sehen 3. Ast 4. Schläfchen 5. Abfall 6. flüstern

Übung 72: 1. are following 2. have worked/have been working 3. believes 4. have had 5. had never broken 6. was living/had been living/came

Übung 73: 1. falsch 2. richtig 3. falsch 4. richtig 5. falsch 6. falsch

Übung 74: 1. onto 2. on 3. of 4. for 5. for 6. at

Übung 75: 1. horse (house) 2. invated (invited) 3. aroun (around) 4. begin (began) 5. securaty (security) 6. dive (drive) 7. shot (short) 8. neeled (kneeled) 9. dificult (difficult)

Übung 76: 1. heulen – wail 2. endlich – finally 3. einsam – lonesome 4. zustimmen – agree 5. schweigsam – silent 6. Gegend – area 7. ängstlich – nervously

Übung 77: 1. The money was stolen by Cinderella. 2. The police were not called by the victim. 3. The car was not driven by Carmody. 4. The novel was worked on during the day (by the author). 5. The car was being driven in the rain (by her). 6. He has been warned by the police.

Übung 78: 1. liver 2. tongue 3. stomach 4. kidneys 5. throat, Lösung: vomit

Übung 79: 1. steak 2. mean 3. contrastingly 4. intimate 5. dawn 6. fizzle

Übung 80: 1. falsch 2. falsch 3. richtig 4. richtig 5. richtig 6. falsch

Übung 81: 1. many 2. some 3. much 4. some 5. few 6. some

Übung 82: 1. diverse 2. banter 3. respond 4. prospective 5. wretched 6. tenderly

Übung 83: 1. robbery 2. traces 3. unlikely 4. complicated 5. final 6. owner 7. food

Übung 84: She/he said: (s)he was having a good time. 2. He/she loved good ice cream. 3. She/he had had that for lunch yesterday. 4. He/she had been worried about that yesterday but he/she wasn't anymore. 5. She/he had been there several times. 6. (That) If I wanted him/her, he/she would be in the garden.

Übung 85: 1. certain 2. believe 3. statement 4. meet 5. so 6. thorough 7. serious 8. in 9. at

Übung 86: 1. Hausangestellte/maid 2. oben/upstairs 3. murrte/grumbled 4. Angebot/offer 5. unwahrscheinlich/unlikely 6. Überredungskunst/powers of persuasion 7. Selbstmitleid/self-pity 8. höhnische Bemerkung/gibe

Übung 87: 1. I drive to work every day. 2. She has been to Paris once or twice. 3. Do not tell him what to do. 4. Why are you so mean? 5. Have you got something to do? 6. You look marvellous, darling.

Übung 88: 1. in 2. on 3. to 4. off 5. into 6. at

Übung 89: 1. within 2. round 3. obviously 4. drive 5. began 6. shoulder 7. pavement 8. breath 9. lawn

Übung 90: 1. zu Pferde 2. reiten 3. Hufeisen 4. Rosshaar 5. Steigbügel 6. Sattel

Übung 91: 1. woke 2. had not called 3. knew 4. are 5. can 6. was 7. had often been 8. became 9. does

Übung 92: 1. a 2. b 3. a 4. c 5. b

Übung 93: 1. interrupting 2. don't know 3. surprise 4. sarcasm 5. quickly 6. imagine 7. disarm

Übung 94: 1. requested 2. up 3. novelist 4. forward 5. away 6. clear 7. in

Übung 95: 1. crafty 2. charitably 3. for once 4. splash 5. dive into 6. back and forth

Übung 96: 1. where to now 2. scarf 3. window 4. knock 5. forehead

Übung 97: 1. to 2. on 3. in 4. out 5. on

Übung 98: 1. He compares it to a disease. 2. He is worried about how well Evers can ride a horse. 3. Carmody is to drive. 4. That's a good question! It is not clear, is it? 5. He has a broken arm and a separated shoulder. 6. No, she doesn't.

Übung 99: 1. She/he said you/I could drive. 2. He/she said that he/she had fallen down and hurt himself/herself. 3. She/he said I should wait for her/him in the car. 4. He/she said he/she would be back in a moment. 5. She/he said she/he had worked with Martin Evers for three years. 6. He/she asked where I went at Christmas time.

Übung 100: 1. portrayal 2. bush 3. credentials 4. siren 5. burglary 6. instantly

Übung 101: 1. c 2. a 3. c 4. b 5. a

Übung 102: 1. had gone wrong 2. had met 3. had simply spiralled 4. knew 5. had never been 6. had done 7. did not look 8. had not done

Übung 103: 1. papers 2. bother 3. real 4. recognize 5. continued 6. mistake 7. questions

Übung 104: 1. in 2. in 3. with 4. of 5. on 6. in 7. of 8. about

Übung 105: 1. this 2. anyone 3. anything 4. an accountant 5. swag 6. find 7. remember 8. hung up 9. house 10. immediately

Lösungen Abschlusstest

Übung 1: 1. pond 2. sensual 3. upset 4. file 5. intimate 6. splash

Übung 2: 1. have known 2. are working 3. drives 4. flew 5. has lived 6. were talking/rang

Übung 3: 1. expert 2. ordinary 3. nervous 4. reluctant 5. important 6. artificial

Übung 4: 1. over 2. on 3. in/of 4. of 5. to 6. away/out

Übung 5: 1. exhausted 2. wound up 3. boundary 4. precise 5. wretched 6. prospective 7. trace 8. proprietor 9. papers 10. think 11. real

Übung 6: 1. He got home late one morning. 2. You have to do something every day. 3. We often go swimming at the weekend. 4. How do you get to work? 5. If you try hard, you will succeed. 6. I have never been to Finland.

Übung 7: 1. surprise 2. effort 3. envelope 4. within 5. vacation 6. forehead

Übung 8: 1. She/he said I was wonderful. 2. He/she said my English had improved quite a bit. 3. She/he said I could always stay with her/him. 4. He/she said (that) if I called him/her, he/she would tell me. 5. She/he said she/he was/had been there yesterday. 6. He/she said she should always do what she was told.

Übung 9: 1. c 2. c 3. a 4. a 5. b 6. a

Übung 10: 1. falsch 2. falsch 3. richtig 4. falsch 5. richtig 6. richtig 7. falsch 8. richtig